22,456

KF
9632
.F55
198

Flemming
Punishment before trial

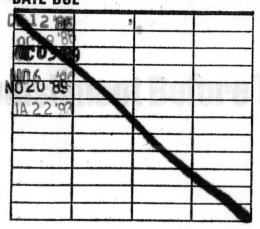

DEMCO

Longman Professional Studies in Law and Public Policy
Editorial Advisor: *Malcolm M. Feeley*

ROY B. FLEMMING *Punishment Before Trial: An Organizational Perspective of Felony Bail Processes*

ROMAN TOMASIC AND MALCOLM M. FEELEY (EDS.) *Neighborhood Justice: An Assessment of an Emerging idea*

Punishment Before Trial

An Organizational Perspective of Felony Bail Processes

Roy B. Flemming
Wayne State University

Longman

New York & London

PUNISHMENT BEFORE TRIAL
An Organizational Perspective of Felony Bail Processes

Longman Inc., 19 West 44th Street, New York, N.Y. 10036
Associated companies, branches, and representatives
throughout the world.

Developmental editor: Irving E. Rockwood
Editorial and Design Supervisor: Joan Matthews
Manufacturing and Production Supervisor: Anne Musso

Table 1.1 adapted from Wayne H. Thomas, Jr., *Bail Reform in America*,
copyright 1969 by The Regents of the University of California;
reprinted by permission of the University of California Press.

Figures 3.1–3.6 and table 3.1 reprinted with permission from Peter F. Nardulli, ed., *The
Study of Criminal Courts: Political Perspectives*, Copyright 1979, Ballinger Publishing
Company.

Library of Congress Cataloging in Publication Data

Flemming, Roy B.
  Punishment before trial.

  (Longman professional studies in law and public
policy)
  Bibliography: p.
  Includes index.
  1. Bail—United States.   2. Pre-trial release—
United States.   3. Bail—Michigan—Detroit.
4. Bail—Maryland—Baltimore.   I. Title.   II. Series.
KF9632.F55   345.72′072   81-17222
ISBN 0-582-28321-3   347.30572   AACR2
ISBN 0-582-28320-5 (pbk.)

Manufactured in the United States of America
        9 8 7 6 5 4 3 2 1

To Toni, who asked the right question first

Contents

Figures and Tables

FIGURES

TABLES

Foreword

In 1961 a young social worker and a wealthy philanthropist initiated the Manhattan Bail Project, an action that sparked a nationwide movement for bail reform. With support provided by Louis Schweitzer, the young social worker, Herbert Sturz, founded the Vera Foundation (later Institute) and initiated a pretrial release project in Manhattan's criminal courts. The idea was deceptively simple: Volunteers interviewed arrestees prior to arraignment and then recommended to the court that those with strong ties to the community be released on their own recognizance (ROR). Publicity generated by this project led the United States Congress and state legislatures across the country to rewrite the laws on pretrial release, and courts in dozens of cities (well over two hundred by last count) created their own pretrial release programs, many of which were patterned after Vera's initial bail project.

This movement has been one of the few clear successes in criminal justice reform during the past two decades. Today throughout the United States arrestees are much more likely to be released than they were twenty-five years ago. Many are now routinely released on their promise to appear. While money bail continues to exist and point up the contradictions inherent in our commitment to equal administration of the law, on average the amounts required are lower than before. No one seriously denies that the bail reform movement has had a significant impact.

But while the results of this movement are evident, the particular causes and conditions for its institutionalized success are more elusive. Perhaps because the initial Manhattan Bail Project met with such success and publicity, there has been a tendency to attribute the success of the movement to the proliferation of agencies like it. Or perhaps because there is a correlation between expansion of such pretrial release agencies and the liberalization of conditions of release, a causal inference has been drawn. Whatever the reasons, this book reveals that the conditions for change in concrete situations vary. A community with liberal laws and a specialized agency may not experience substantial change, while one without them may. Roy Flemming's study reveals the importance of context and the necessity of political power to effect change. Rules and administrative structures alone are insufficient. Indeed they may be counter-productive in that they provide the appearance of change without the sub-stance, and they may lull a concerned public into quiescence. By carefully examining the history, process, and impact of bail reform in two com-munities, Baltimore and Detroit, Flemming reveals the types of concrete actions that must accompany good intentions if innovations are to be effective.

The study does much more. Like other recent research Flemming's study shows that what occurs in the courts is dependent in part upon fac-tors outside its control, and in so doing reveals how courts are not always what they appear to be. For instance, he finds that bail in Baltimore is on average several hundred dollars higher than bail in Detroit, a fact which might lead a casual observer to conclude that Detroit is more "progres-sive" than Baltimore. But Flemming's study reveals a number of other off-setting factors: The bondsman's fee is substantially lower in Baltimore than Detroit, and there is more competition among them in Baltimore. The pretrial release agency in Baltimore is timid, and the black commun-ity there is not as well organized as Detroit's. Despite its lack of programs to affect ROR, the Detroit jail had been the object of a successful law suit challenging its capacity and conditions. And so on.

This is not to suggest that specialized pretrial release agencies are un-important or unnecessary. Indeed, their very presence in many of the na-tion's major cities may be what keeps the concern with liberalized pretrial release on the agenda to criminal justice officials, who all too often jump from one fad to another in a search for solutions to the continuing "crisis" that faces the courts.

As policy analysis, this book is valuable because it reveals the nature and extent of political activity required to mobilize legal change. This is particularly important, for many people, and especially lawyers, view change in and through the legal process as an *alternative* to politics. As a text for reformers, this study is valuable in that it reveals that language, structure, and administrative procedure are secondary to mobilization of powerful supporters. As a study of the impact of court decisions, this book reveals in concrete detail the power of the courts to effect social change when their rulings are coupled with organized political follow up. As a study of race, crime, and urban politics, this study reveals the im-portance of strategically placed black elites in ameliorating the lingering and pervasive effects of racial discrimination.

It is then for several audiences, and because of the author's style and skill, it is accessible to them all.

Malcolm M. Feeley

Preface

I first started looking into bail nearly 10 years ago by spending a few evenings with the commissioners in Baltimore to see if there was anything interesting about what they were doing. At the time, my days were devoted to observing the disposition of felony cases in the city's criminal court. Bail in comparison seemed far from being as glamorous. My thoughts about bail also had been formed by two reactions to what I had read of the existing literature. First, it rarely told me how bail decisions were made from the perspective of those who made them. Second, there just was not any theoretical bite to the research. The underlying reason was that study after study was dominated by a concern over reform that either pointed to problems without explaining why they existed, or attempted to evaluate particular reforms without expressing an interest in asking, much less taking the time to say, why this particular court reformed its bail policies while others had not. To be frank, there was some doubt whether there was any need for yet another bail study if it followed the same path as those preceding it. The time spent with the commissioners convinced me there was a need. The question was finding a different route.

As my notes about bail hearings and interviews began to accumulate, however, I soon discovered I was caught in something of a dilemma created in part by the atheoretical character of the literature. What was it that needed explaining, and how could it be explained best? For a while I dodged the problem by recording in as much detail as possible what I observed and found out through the interviews and conversations with officials. But it became apparent that I would have to make a decision that Camus in *The Myth of Sisyphus* described as "the choice between a description that is sure but that teaches me nothing and hypotheses that claim to teach me but that are not sure."

The theoretical perspective of this book resulted from my efforts to solve this problem and reflects my attempt to get a larger sense of what I saw and learned in the courtrooms. As it evolved, it took on a dual role. One aspect was to provide a systematic explanation of why bail policies differed in Baltimore and Detroit; the other was to explain why they

changed. In the end, I found I was working on the problems in the literature that had bothered me in the first place. Unfortunately, even after 10
years, little theoretical development has occurred in the study of bail. My
hope is that this book points the way for others, for punishment before
trial poses critical problems for American criminal courts.

The opportunity to conduct this study I owe entirely to James Eisenstein and to Herbert Jacob. They asked me to go to Baltimore to work on
the *Felony Justice* project, encouraged me in my work, shared the project's sample data, and commented on the study in its various forms.
Herb's confidence in me has been a source of pleasure. My relationship
with Jim has changed over the years from TA to colleague and friend. He
has taught me a lot about teaching, critiquing papers, and interviewing
judges who say, "I only have a few minutes. What do you want to
know?"

Tom Anton supervised this study when it was a thesis. He was wise
enough to know when I really needed help and I thank him for it. I also
want to thank Milton Heumann, who pointed out to me that I had something here; Peter Nardulli, who by happenstance read the thesis and gave
me a chance to draw out more clearly the dynamics of change that had
been embedded in the Detroit case study; and John Kingdon for his comments. Bryan D. Jones returned a favor by reading this manuscript in its
penultimate form and caused me to reconsider what I had done. Finally,
Joan M. Mathews typed this manuscript with a professionalism that I
hope it deserves.

I think it also is appropriate to acknowledge a debt to Forrest Dill
who recommended publication of this manuscript. His death this past
summer saddened all who learned something new about bondsmen because of his research.

Portions of Chapters 2 and 3 first appeared as "Punishment Before
Trial: A Political Choice Model of Policy Changes in Pretrial Sanction-
ing" in Peter F. Nardulli (ed.) *The Study of Criminal Courts: Political
Perpectives*, Cambridge Ballinger Publishing Company, 1979.

Roy B. Flemming

Punishment Before Trial

1

Introduction

PUNISHMENT BEFORE TRIAL: A STATEMENT OF THE PROBLEM

Sitting in chambers with the prosecutor and attorney shortly after the noon recess for lunch, the judge announced that the first order of business when court reconvened would be a motion to reduce bail filed by a defendant recently indicted by Baltimore's grand jury for burglary. By doing this, the judge said, the rest of the afternoon would be cleared to start an unexpected jury trial in an armed robbery case that the prosecutor and public defender had told him earlier that morning might be a guilty plea. Negotiations had broken down, however. Now the judge was anxious to begin so he would not fall too far behind his docket. Sounds from the busy street in front of the ornate Supreme Bench courthouse filtered into the wood paneled courtroom lined with dark portraits of deceased jurists and created a murmuring background to the proceedings that began when the judge took his place behind the raised dais to hear the bail motion.

Ostensibly, the purpose of bail is to assure the appearance of criminal defendants at their hearings and trial, and there are constitutional guarantees that bail should not be excessive.[1] All of this is consistent with the presumption of innocence that forms the basis for due process in American criminal courts. Other issues are at stake, however, and they are especially evident in criminal cases involving citizens accused of committing felony crimes. Whether a defendant will attempt to evade justice is just one of several concerns courts feel compelled to consider in deciding the conditions effecting the release of defendants from custody. Among these considerations, a key concern focuses on whether the defendant will commit additional crimes if released or threaten the safety of others. The presumption of innocence, already tainted by the fact that the defendant has been arrested for a felony crime, thus clashes with the court's responsibility for assuring the well-being of the community. That

1

afternoon in the early seventies, an observer waiting to watch a jury trial, the apotheosis of American criminal justice, also would have seen the realities of the dilemmas inherent in how its bail system operates.

Since the defendant had filed his own motion for a bail reduction, he had to argue the merits of his case before the judge without benefit of counsel. At his arraignment, a lower court official had set a $6,000 surety bond for his release. He had been arrested and later indicted for two burglaries allegedly committed while on probation for a larceny conviction. The defendant told the judge he previously had been released pending trial and had made all his court appearances. He asked for a bail reduction because he could not afford a bail over $2,000. After the judge stated that he thought the existing bail was reasonable, the following exchange took place.

> JUDGE: *Two serious charges? I have to consider the protection of society, that sort of thing.*
>
> DEF.: *I thought I was supposed to be innocent until proven guilty?*
>
> JUDGE: *If I thought that I'd release you on recognizance. No, I can't do that. Maybe sometime if they change the law, but not right now.*

In the end, the judge, balancing his various concerns about the defendant, split the difference between the existing and requested bail amounts and reduced the bail to $4,000.

This book is about the dilemmas criminal court officials face when deciding whether felony defendants should be freed pending trial and how they are solved. The issue is a fundamental one in American criminal justice because the resolution of these dilemmas often leads to the punishment of citizens who have yet to be tried for the crimes they are alleged to have committed. The defendant who requested a bail reduction, for example, already had been detained for several weeks in the Baltimore City Jail. If he did not make the lower bail, the chances were good he would stay in jail for several more weeks before his case was heard by the court. In the event that he had money for bail, he paid a surety bondsman at least $270 to have him post the bond. Punishment before trial, then, shares the same features as sentencing following conviction. Defendants lose their liberty, spend time in jail, and incur financial penalties. What distinguishes them, of course, is the finding of guilt through legal processes that forges the link between crime and punishment. At the time bail conditions are imposed or reconsidered, this link is missing.[2] As a matter of public policy and legal principle, therefore, if the presumption of innocence is to have substantive meaning, the scope and cost of pretrial sanctioning should be minimized for the maximum number of defendants.

Punishment before trial varies in large measure according to the choices criminal courts make from an array of pretrial release options. Its scope depends upon the frequency with which courts release defendants on their own recognizance at the time of their initial bail hearing. Recognizance release and other forms of conditional release do not impose financial penalties on defendants because they are freed on their promise to appear in court.[3] Criminal penalties may result if they do fail to appear, and in many courts they are released under the supervision of agencies charged with the responsibility for assuring their court appearance. Since punishment occurs when defendants are detained or incur financial losses by posting money bail, the scope of pretrial punishment becomes narrower as the frequency of recognizance release increases at initial bail hearings. Conversely, the scope broadens if they are granted infrequently. Clearly, the use of recognizance release at the earliest possible stage in the criminal disposition process is critical in shaping the potential punitiveness of felony bail policies. As the scope of pretrial policies expands, more defendants are likely to pay a price for their liberty, be detained in jail, or both.

The severity or cost of pretrial sanctions depends on a number of factors. Financial costs reflect the type of money bail and its size or amount. The most common form of money bail is surety bail. When sureties are required by a court, the defendant must pay a bondsman a nonrefundable premium based on a certain percentage of the total amount and possibly provide collateral in the form of personal property to secure his or her release. The bondsman then posts a surety bond with the court with the stipulation that if the defendant fails to appear in court, the bond will be forfeited and the bondsman will pay the court the full amount of the bond. Accordingly, the bondsman is presumed to have a financial incentive to guarantee the defendant's presence in court. A second form of cash bail is called variously security bond, deposit bail, or percentage bail. Defendants with these bonds deposit usually 10 percent of the amount directly with the court instead of paying a bondsman. At the conclusion of the case, if the defendant has attended all the proceedings, the deposit is returned to the defendant.[4] Failure to appear may bring both criminal penalties and forfeiture of the total bond. Financial costs, then, vary directly with the size of the bond and may be either permanent in the case of surety bails or temporary in the instance of security bonds.

A second aspect of the costs of pretrial punishment is the detention of defendants and the length of time they stay in jail. Incarceration occurs when defendants are unable to raise the money to make either security or surety bail because they lack the financial wherewithal to do so or the bond amounts are simply too high. How long defendants stay in jail depends on how quickly their families or friends can collect the money needed for their bail and how swiftly the court processes its caseload. Detention also occurs when state laws allow local courts to deny defendants the opportunity to post bail and remand them directly to the jail because of the gravity of their charge, generally crimes of violence such as homicide. In criminal courts, for example, where cash bails regardless of type are high, remands are frequent, and the pace with which cases are concluded is slow, the chances of pretrial detention are high, and the periods of incarceration long.

The breadth and severity of pretrial punishment ultimately reflect a complex mixture of influences flowing from initial bail setting policies, changes in these decisions because of motions for bail reduction, the economic resources of defendants, business practices of bondsmen, state laws, and the pace at which courts complete their cases. The problem of whom to release and how is thus enmeshed in a larger context. One thing is clear, however, the scope and cost of pretrial punishment vary widely in American criminal courts, as indicated by Table 1.1, which is based on a survey of 20 cities in 1971, shortly before this study began.

TABLE 1.1   Pretrial Release Policies for Felony Defendants in 1971

Proportion Detained Through Disposition (Median = 34 Percent)	Proportion Released on Recognizance Prior to Disposition (Median = 18 Percent)	
	Below Median	Above Median
Above Median	Houston (2;34) Kansas City (3;63) Chicago (11;42) Boston (13;62) Wilmington (14;39) Los Angeles (17;38) San Francisco (17;44) Hartford (18;37) Oakland (18;49)	Sacramento (30;36)
Below Median	Denver (13;23) Minneapolis (14;13)	Peoria (19;28) San Jose (26;33) Philadelphia (33;20) Champaign-Urbana (37;19) Detroit (37;30) San Diego (45;26) Des Moines (47;21) Washington, D.C. (56;31)

SOURCE: Adapted from Wayne H. Thomas, Jr., *Bail Reform in America*, (Berkeley: University of California, 1976), Table 3, p. 41.
NOTE: Numbers in parentheses indicate recognizance and detention rates, respectively.

The proportion of felony defendants freed on recognizance and the percentage detained for the entire pretrial period are two important indicators of the punitiveness of bail policies. The median recognizance rate for the 20 cities in 1971 was 18 percent and the median detention rate was 34 percent. By sorting the cities according to whether their rates fell below or above these medians, two major policy clusters were formed.

In the upper left corner of the table, in what might be labeled the "more punitive" cluster, were nine cities with an average recognizance release rate of 13 percent and an average detention rate of 45 percent. Use of recognizance release for felony defendants ranged from rare, as in Houston and Kansas City, to relatively infrequent as in Oakland and Hartford. The likelihood of pretrial detention was comparatively high in seven of these cities, but none came close to Kansas City or Boston where nearly two-thirds of the felony defendants remained in jail until the courts disposed of their charges.

The lower right corner of the table, the "less punitive" cluster, includes cities where the scope of pretrial sanctioning was narrower and the odds of being jailed before trial were lower. For these eight cities, recognizance releases averaged 38 percent of the defendants and the proportion of detained defendants averaged 26 percent. Washington, D.C. released the highest proportion of defendants on recognizance with over half of its felony defendants freed in this manner. Among the larger cities in this group Philadelphia had the lowest detention rate with a fifth of its felony defendants jailed pending trial.

Pretrial release policies involving felony defendants clearly differed markedly among these cities in 1971. Equally significant is the fact that these policies varied in their relative stability. Overall, according to the same study that provided the information for Table 1.1, the average recognizance rate for the 20 cities rose from 5 percent in 1962 to 23 percent in 1971, and the average detention rate fell from 53 percent to 34 percent.[5] Cities in the more punitive cluster in 1971, however, had made smaller changes in their policies during this ten-year span than the cities in the less punitive cluster.[6]

For example, Boston, Houston, and Kansas City, all of which were in the more punitive policy grouping, showed little or no change regarding recognizance release. In Boston the proportion of defendants released through this bail option was 12.4 percent in 1962 and 12.8 percent in 1971. In 1962 no defendants in Houston were granted recognizance, and the proportion was a mere 1.2 percent in Kansas City. By 1971 the rates were at best marginally higher. Detention rates tended to follow the same pattern. In both 1962 and 1971 Boston detained 60 percent of its felony defendants, while in Houston the proportion remained steady at about one-third. For Kansas City the rate dropped from 78 percent to 63 percent. In sharp contrast, cities in the less punitive cluster in 1971 generally had experienced dramatic shifts in both rates. For example, recognizance release went from less than 5 percent to nearly 45 percent in San Diego, and in Washington, D.C. the proportion leapt from 0 to over 55 percent. Detention rates correspondingly plummetted in both cities. In San Diego the rate fell from about 67 percent in 1962 to about 26 percent ten years later, and in Washington the rate dropped from 61 to 31 percent.

It is plainly evident that criminal courts decide whether and how to free felony defendants prior to trial in different ways, and that these policy solutions vary in their stability. Why are the pretrial release policies of some courts more punitive than others? What are the conditions fostering stability or change in these policies and their outcomes for defendants? This book seeks to answer these questions and by doing so to develop a better understanding of how punishment before trial emerges through the American bail system. It presents a comparative study of two criminal courts whose felony bail policies in 1972 approximated the two policy clusters found in Table 1.1. Because of the importance of initial bail-setting decisions in shaping outcomes for defendants, it focuses most intently on this stage in the disposition process. To guide the analysis of these courts, a conceptual framework that integrates both the context and process of pretrial release decision making is developed. Since considerable changes in the scope and costs of pretrial sanctioning occurred in one court, a model of policy change based on the framework is outlined and then later elaborated in the case studies. Finally, the role of bondsmen is investigated in recognition of the fact that the outcomes of pretrial release policies often depend on their decisions. In order to lay a basis for the subsequent case studies, an overview of the two cities will be useful at this point.

AN OVERVIEW OF BAIL PROCEDURES AND POLICIES IN DETROIT AND BALTIMORE

The empirical basis for this book rests on detailed case studies of pretrial release practices in Detroit and Baltimore.[7] In 1972 when sample data for roughly 1,500 felony defendants in each city were collected, their policies were sufficiently different that they resembled other cities in the policy clusters discussed earlier. While the two cities cannot be treated as representative of the cities in the groupings, by the same token they did not occupy a narrow band of the policy spectrum.

In terms of the two dimensions of pretrial punishment defining the policy clusters, Detroit was less punitive than Baltimore. Detroit's criminal court freed nearly 49 percent of the sampled felony defendants on their own recognizance after their initial bail hearing, a rate exceeded only by Washington, D.C. in 1971. Moreover, as Table 1.1 indicates, Detroit's proportion of defendants released on recognizance in 1972 had increased over the previous year's rate. This court's detention rate of 32 percent, however, was higher than most of the cities in the less punitive cluster. In Baltimore during 1972 recognizance was granted less frequently to felony defendants. The proportion released in this manner was slightly less than 12 percent. Its detention rate correspondingly was higher at 41 percent. Both rates put Baltimore roughly in the middle of the cities that made up the more punitive policy group.

This overview was two purposes. First, it briefly sketches the outlines of the bail procedures, the extent of reform, and the basic court structure in the two cities. As will be seen shortly, the pretrial release policies were not consistent with the amount of bail reform that had taken place in the courts. Second, before the analysis can proceed, it is necessary to consider the possibility that the policy differences between the cities were spurious or artifacts of underlying differences in the criminal charges lodged against defendants. This discussion will also suggest that efforts to establish the correlates of pretrial release decisions may offer limited understanding of why the substance of pretrial release policies differs.

Bail Procedures in the Two Cities

The two courts, their bail procedures, and the officials involved in the proceedings were quite different. Detroit's court was structurally unified and geographically centralized. Its bail procedures and rules were relatively unreformed, and the court's judges were responsible for setting bails in addition to their other tasks. In contrast, Baltimore had a bifurcated court structure with autonomous lower and upper courts, and the lower court was geographically decentralized. Its bail rules had been reformed by 1972 with a specialized group of officials assigned to conduct bail hearings. Finally, the city had a large, well-established pretrial release agency.

Recorder's Court had sole jurisdiction over felony cases in Detroit. Bail hearings were held in conjunction with the defendant's formal arraignment on the charge. The proceedings took place in a single courtroom before one of the court's 13 judges in the Frank Murphy Hall of Justice located near downtown Detroit. The judges normally rotated this responsibility because they also handled preliminary hearings, guilty pleas, trials, and other proceedings in the criminal disposition process. Formal bail reviews were not regularly scheduled; instead, they were held when requested by attorneys or prosecutors and after the court's recognizance program had determined that a bail reduction might be in order for a detained defendant.

Recorder's Court established a Release on Recognizance Program in 1971 and later made it a division of the court's probation department in 1973. With only 15 employees, almost all of whom were law students working part-time, it was a relatively small agency. Moreover, the program's investigators did not interview defendants prior to arraignment nor did they participate in bail hearings. Instead, its limited personnel concentrated on interviewing defendants detained after their bail hearings to see if they could be released on personal bond (as recognizance was called in Detroit) or when motions for bail reductions had been filed.

Criminal cases were processed by two separate, distinct court systems in Baltimore. Felony defendants, as well as misdemeanor defendants, were arraigned and had their bails set in the city's lower court which become part of Maryland's state-wide district court system in 1971. Twenty-seven commissioners appointed by the chief judge of the court were responsible for making these initial bail determinations. If defendants were not released from custody or failed to post money bail following these hearings, their pretrial release conditions were reviewed generally within a day or so by District Court judges who also presided over preliminary examinations of felony cases. In the event probable cause was found and defendants were indicted by the grand jury, jurisdiction was assumed by Baltimore's Supreme Bench where bail could be reviewed after motions or petitions for bail reduction had been made.

Baltimore's pretrial release procedures and the rules governing bail had undergone two reforms by 1972. Earlier, in 1966, under the auspices of the State's Attorney Office, an assistant prosecutor started a bail project copied after the pioneering Manhattan Bail Project.[8] In 1968 the Supreme Bench adopted the program, set up a three-judge panel to supervise it, and recreated it as its Pre-Trial Release Division. The agency's responsibilities included interviewing defendants prior to bail hearings and for bail reduction motions, recommending for recognizance those who qualified under its rules, and monitoring defendants released under its custody during the pretrial period to assure their appearance in court. By 1972 the agency had grown from a handful of volunteers in 1966 to over 40 full-time employees.

A second, potentially far-reaching reform took place when the rules for Maryland's District Court went into effect in 1971. A new bail rule, Rule 777, reaffirmed the right to release pending trial for all defendants except those charged with offenses then punishable by death. It laid down detailed rules to guide the pretrial release deliberations of the commissioners; mandated automatic bail reviews for defendants detained after their arraignment; eliminated bail schedules to assure individualization of bail decisions; and authorized security bonds or deposit bail as substitutes for surety bonds at the discretion of the commissioners. Equally important, Rule 777 included a presumption that defendants would be released on recognizance:

> Any defendant charged with an offense not punishable by death shall, at his appearance before a judicial officer, be ordered released pending trial on his personal recognizance unless the officer determines that such a release will not reasonably assure the appearance of the defendant as required.

The only criterion governing the release of criminal defendants was their likelihood of appearing in court. There was no provision under the rule that allowed commissioners to take into account, at least explicitly, whether a defendant might pose a danger to the community. Defendants charged with crimes carrying the death penalty in 1971, however, could be denied bail or remanded. No rule in Michigan at the time of this study provided for the use of security bonds or included the presumption that defendants would be released on their own recognizance.

Bail Setting Policies in the Two Cities

Although Baltimore's bail rules and procedures had been reformed more extensively than those in Detroit, its pretrial release policies were more stringent and costlier. Recognizance release, as noted earlier, seldom was granted felony defendants at their arraignment. Its cash bails were also higher, and bail was denied more frequently by Baltimore's commissioners. As Table 1.2 indicates, with recognizance tightly rationed in Baltimore, over 75 percent of the felony defendants were required to post cash bails if they hoped to regain their pretrial liberty, and, despite Rule 777, over 93 percent of these bails were surety bonds. Furthermore, the price set for pretrial freedom was considerably higher, as indicated by the median bail of $4,650, than in Detroit, where the median bail amount was less than half this amount. Finally, almost 13 percent of the felony defendants in Baltimore were remanded compared to just 3 percent in Detroit.[9]

TABLE 1.2   Bail Setting Policies for Felony Defendants in Detroit and Baltimore

	Percent of Defendants	
Bail Decision	Detroit	Baltimore
Recognizance release	48.8	11.8
Cash Bails	48.2	75.3
Remands	3.0	12.9
Total	100.0	100.0
Median Cash Bail	$2,000	$4,650
Number	1536	1676

The two courts obviously had very different bail policies in 1972. Before this conclusion can be accepted, however, the possibility must be explored that the differences may be somewhat illusory simply because the defendants were not similar in terms of such key characteristics as the nature of the criminal charges lodged against them. Without exception, previous studies have found the most important variable associated with the choice of various release options and the size of cash bails is the formal charge.[10] An important facet of this association is that the stringency of pretrial release decisions or the extent of pretrial sanctioning is directly or positively related to the severity or seriousness of the charge. Thus, the likelihood of recognizance release declines and bail amounts increase as charges become more serious. As a result, pretrial release policies might register merely the crime patterns of cities as they are filtered through the enforcement priorities of police departments and the charging policies of the police or prosecutor, depending on who has final say over these decisions.

In both Detroit and Baltimore, variance in the punitiveness of pretrial release conditions was correlated most highly with the defendant's charge.[11] Moreover, the coefficients measuring this association were nearly identical. In Detroit the coefficient was .56 while it was .55 in Baltimore. Adding other variables did not change these results. For example, the multiple correlation coefficient in Detroit rose to only .62 when the existence of a prior record and whether there were additional charges levied against defendants were considered in tandem with the formal charge. For both citites, then, the defendant's formal charge functioned as a major cue in the initial decision regarding the type of bail or release option.

When cash bails were imposed, the formal charges lodged against defendants once again figured prominently in the decision regarding their amounts, although the statistical association was not as strong as in the decision between release alternatives. For Detroit the correlation coefficient was .41 between bail amounts and charges. Efforts to improve upon the size of this coefficient by adding other variables were unsuccessful. In each instance, the coefficients barely exceeded the original one. The results were a bit different in Baltimore. On the one hand, when taken by itself, the charge variable had a coefficient of .38, comparable to Detroit, but when the number of additional similar charges lodged against defendants was included, the coefficient climbed to .57. No other variables in combination with the charge variable produced this high a coefficient.[12]

It bears noting here that the amount of variance that can be attributed to the charge variable was not especially large for either city. Squaring the correlation coefficient in the case of bail choices indicates that approximately 30 percent of the variance in this decision was accounted for by the defendants' formal charges. The amount of explained variance was even smaller when turning to cash bail amounts. Approximately 16 percent of the variance in the Detroit sample and 14 percent in Baltimore could be assigned to the influence of the charge variables. Nonetheless, these results are consistent with other analyses.[13]

With the sample data indicating that bail decisions in both cities were associated most strongly with the defendant's charge, it is time to turn to a comparison of the kinds of bail defendants with roughly similar charges received in Baltimore and Detroit. The following table compares by charge the proportion of defendants granted recognizance release at their initial bail hearings.

TABLE 1.3   Recognizance Release by Charge in Detroit and Baltimore

Major Charge at Arraignment	Percent of Defendants Released on Recognizance at Arraignment (Number)			
	Detroit		Baltimore	
Weapon	75.2	(266)	—	
Drug-Related Crime				
Heroin Possession	72.1	(122)	15.4	(13)
Dist. Misc. Drugs	47.9	(48)	7.5	(67)
Dist. Heroin	50.0	(26)	5.0	(199)
Property Crime				
Theft	47.5	(177)	38.4	(138)
Burglary	46.5	(170)	13.9	(373)
Personal Victim Crime				
Assault	56.2	(118)	12.9	(62)
Robbery	31.7	(41)	12.3	(219)
Armed Robbery	3.1	(159)	2.6	(271)
Rape	4.8	(21)	2.4	(85)
Murder	5.5	(54)	10.2	(65)
Other	57.8	(249)	14.5	(179)
Average	48.8	(1,536)	11.8	(1,676)

The decisions made in Baltimore were more stringent, regardless of the charge, than those made in Detroit. The highest proportion of recognizance releases for defendants in Baltimore involved those accused of such relatively minor felonies as theft or larceny. About 38 percent of these defendants were freed by commissioners in this manner compared to 47 percent by Detroit's judges. Defendants charged with more serious property crimes such as burglary in Detroit's court fared almost as well as those arraigned on theft charges; 46 percent of them were granted personal bonds. In contrast, the proportion was only 14 percent in Baltimore. For crimes involving personal victims, such as aggravated assault, roughly 56 percent of the defendants were released in Detroit compared to Baltimore's 13 percent. Only when the charges were extremely serious did bail choices in the two courts resemble one another. For example, 3 percent of Detroit's armed robbery defendants and about the same percent in Baltimore received recognizance bails. Still, when viewed overall, the scope of pretrial punishment was considerably broader in Baltimore than in Detroit for most felony crimes.

The median and mean amounts of cash bails imposed in each court paralleled their differences in the use of recognizance release, as shown in Table 1.4. The commissioners' reluctance to choose recognizance was not mitigated by the size of the bonds they required as conditions for release. In this sense, the severity of their decisions exceeded those made in Detroit since defendants in Baltimore in the aggregate had to pay more for their release, and, as its relatively higher detention rate indicated earlier, they were more likely to be detained until the court disposed of their cases. Table 1.4 shows that with the exception of rape and murder cases, where the number of defendants is quite small because most of them were remanded, Baltimore's median bail amounts exceeded those in Detroit by amounts ranging from $500 to $4,500. Average bails in Baltimore were higher also across most charge categories.

TABLE 1.4   Median and Mean Cash Bail Amounts by Charge in Detroit and Baltimore

Major Arraignment Charge	Median Cash Bail				Mean Cash Bail	
	Detroit		Baltimore		Detroit	Baltimore
Weapon	$ 500	(66)			$1,560	
Drug-Related Crime						
Heroin Poss.	750	(34)	4,000	(11)	1,850	4,090
Misc. Drug Dist.	2,500	(25)	3,500	(61)	2,820	5,420
Dist. Heroin	1,500	(13)	6,000	(180)	7,230	9,270
Property Crime						
Theft	1,000	(93)	1,500	(85)	1,650	5,530
Burglary	1,000	(91)	3,000	(312)	1,670	3,870
Personal Victim Crime						
Assault	2,500	(50)	7,000	(43)	4,930	11,580
Robbery	2,000	(28)	5,000	(184)	2,510	6,210
Armed Robbery	5,000	(154)	8,000	(241)	8,080	20,520
Rape	5,000	(20)	4,000	(7)	6,920	23,860
Murder	5,000	(11)	2,500	(7)	6,680	29,990
Other	2,500	(102)	2,000	(124)	4,790	3,910
Overall	$2,000	(740)	$4,650	(1,261)	$4,500	$8,920

To summarize, both courts relied on the formal charges lodged against defendants to guide their determination of pretrial release conditions. In addition, these conditions tended to be more stringent and costlier for defendants when their charges were serious. What must be highlighted, however, is the fact that despite similarities in decision rules or cues, the scope and severity of pretrial release policies differed between the two cities for reasons other than the nature of the charge. Felony defendants who might be released on their own recognizance in Detroit were much more likely to face the need to post a surety bond, often of substantial size, in Baltimore. Thus, the *content* of the decisions, although shaped by similar considerations regarding the gravity of the offense, was dissimilar in the two courts.

CONCLUSIONS

Deciding whom to release at what price and whom to detain pending trial pose critical problems for American criminal justice because the presumed innocence of citizens accused of crimes, and its corollary of the right to nonexcessive bail, conflict with the equally strong presumption that society's safety and well-being are affected by the actions of its courts. This problem admits no easy solution, and it becomes even more acute when felony crimes violating basic social norms and values are involved. Court officials, nevertheless, must make choices every day that, deliberately or not, result in a balance between these competing demands. The nature of the charge provides some guidance in making these choices. The critical feature that needs to be reemphasized, however, is that the content of choices involving defendants accused of roughly similar crimes differs from one court to another. How can these differences be explained?

A focus concentrating only on the decision process and the correlates of decisions would lose sight of the central fact that the scope and costs of bail policies are influenced by political and institutional factors that determine the feasibility of pretrial punishment. All defendants are unlikely to be freed on recognizance at their arraignment because the wholesale release of those accused of rape, murder, or armed robbery would be politically unfeasible regardless of their likelihood of appearing in court. Nor can all of them be incarcerated; jails in large cities rarely are big enough. Between these two improbable extremes, criminal courts fashion policies through the liberal or stringent employment of recognizance bail and higher or lower bail amounts that satisfy political exigencies within the constraints set by local detention resources. As a result, these policies not only lead to the pretrial punishment of defendants, they also affect other individuals and groups in the community. Public officials, citizen groups, local media, members of the criminal justice establishment, and bondsmen all may perceive themselves as gaining or losing material benefits or symbolic gratification through these policies. The political environment of criminal courts as reflected in the context of choice for bail decisions, therefore, is an important vantage point from which to search for the reasons why policies differ and how they change.

The following chapter introduces the conceptual framework used in this study. It stresses the political difficulties and the uncertainties court officials confront in making bail decisions for felony defendants. It also highlights the role of resources, particularly jails, in creating or limiting the range of choices available to courts. A second facet of this framework is that it suggests that the problems of deciding what is a proper decision or excessive bail are simplified by officials by relying on the precedents incorporated into a court's "bail tariff." It then identifies the conditions for different modes of choice or ways in which decisions typically are made. The framework, then, integrates both context and process in order to understand why the contents of policies differ. The models of change that build on this framework take up the issue of determining the conditions under which the substance of these policies is most likely to change and how.

The framework presented in Chapter 2, then, provides a systematic scheme for answering the questions raised in this book. It offers a means of explaining why court policies differ and maps the dynamics of change. After this chapter, the case studies of Detroit and Baltimore are presented, as well as an investigation of the outcomes of these policies. In the concluding chapter, the dilemmas of how punishment before trial can be minimized will be addressed by looking at the implications of this book's theoretical perspective and its findings for bail reform.

REFERENCES

1. A good review of current laws and policies regarding bail in the United States can be found in John S. Goldkamp, *Two Classes of Accused: A Study of Bail and Detention in American Justice*, Cambridge, Ballinger Publishing Company, 1979. As Goldkamp's discussion makes clear the constitutional guarantees surrounding bail are not absolute.
2. Herbert L. Packer, *The Limits of the Criminal Sanction*, Stanford, Stanford University Press, 1968.
3. See Wayne H. Thomas, Jr., *Bail Reform in America*, Berkeley, University of California Press, 1976, for a discussion of various nonfinancial release methods and how they operate.
4. In some states and local jurisdictions, a portion of the deposit is deducted before it is refunded to defendants to defray the administrative costs of the bail system; see Thomas, *Bail Reform in America*, for further discussion of this bail option. In Chicago, the deposit generally was assigned to pay attorney fees; see James Eisenstein and Herbert Jacob, *Felony Justice: An Organizational Analysis of Criminal Courts*, Boston, Little, Brown and Company, 1977, p. 120.
5. Thomas, *Bail Reform in America*, pp. 40–41.
6. Using the information from Thomas for 1962 and 1971, and sorting the cities according to whether the amount of change in the two rates exceeded or fell below the medians, created groupings of cities that were similar but not identical to those shown in Table 1.1. See Thomas, *Bail Reform in America*, pp. 40–41.
7. See the appendix to this book for a description of the research methods and data sources used in this study.
8. A history of this seminal reform is presented by Lee S. Friedman, "The Evolution of Bail Reform," *Policy Sciences*, 7 (September 1976): 281–313.
9. A major reason for this difference was that Maryland laws allowed court officials to remand defendants accused of murder, arson, rape, and kidnapping.

Only homicide defendants in Michigan could be denied bail at the time of the study.

10. The statistical relationship between formal charges and bail decisions has been demonstrated in numerous studies. For a comprehensive review of this literature, see National Center for State Courts, *An Evaluation of Policy Related Research on the Effectiveness of Pre-Trial Release Programs*, Denver, National Center for State Courts, 1975.

11. The primary purpose of this discussion is to establish whether or not the policy differences between the cities can be dismissed as largely functions of defendant characteristics. Accordingly, the discussion is kept brief. There are, however, several points that should be kept in mind.

First, the charge variable is actually the set of charge categories treated as dichotomous variables in the first stage of the process. This means that the correlation coefficient referred to in the text is a multiple correlation coefficient. Second, the dependent variable was operationalized as an ordinal ranking of the options according to their punitiveness with recognizance ranked as least punitive and remands as most punitive. If this variable is operationalized in other ways the overall conclusion regarding the importance of the charge variable remains intact, although the results differ for the cities.

If the variable is defined as the choice between recognizance and cash bail (a dichotomous dummy variable), the multiple correlation coefficient is .29 for Baltimore and .44 in Detroit. These coefficients rise to .36 and .52 respectively when a prior record variable, also a dummy variable, is added to the regression equation. If the dependent variable is defined as a choice between remand and other bail types (cash bail and recognizance), the coefficient is .69 for Baltimore and .81 in Detroit. The prior record dummy variable does not increase the size of these coefficients if it is added; nor did any other defendant-related variables available from the data make any change in the coefficients. These results tentatively suggest that in Detroit "criminality" may have been more important than in Baltimore; a conclusion consistent with the nature of the bail process in Detroit examined in Chapter 3 where because of severe jail problems the judges had to release large numbers of defendants and hence the role of charge and record played perhaps a greater role in the decision process. In Baltimore where the decision process was less constrained by jail resources and the decision process was less routine than in Detroit and more "situational," other factors than the charge against defendants could enter into the decisions. Chapter 4 gives greater detail regarding the decision process in Baltimore.

A third matter needing clarification is the operationalization of the charge variable in the second stage of the process. When the cash amounts were arrayed by charge according to their rank order of seriousness following the data given by Rossi, et al. (see Peter H. Rossi, et al., "The Seriousness of Crimes: Normative Structures and Individual Differences," *American Sociological Review*, 39 (April 1974): 224–237), the distributions were curvilinear in each city with amounts rising sharply as charges became more serious, implying or suggesting that the charges did not increase in perceived importance in uniform or equal increments. The variables consequently were transformed by squaring the numerical rank value of the charge in Detroit and cubing them in Baltimore; the reason for this difference being greater curvilinearity in Baltimore's distribution. The charge variable, therefore, is not a set of dichotomous variables as in the first stage and the simple correlation coefficient measures the importance of charge in setting cash bail amounts.

12. It remains an open question whether these results could be enhanced by more information and more refined measures of defendant backgrounds. It is more likely that they indicate the limits of what Hogarth calls the "black box model" of decision making in courts. He also found relatively small coefficients when only the factual characteristics of defendants were treated as the primary factors in sentencing decisions. See John Hogarth, *Sentencing as a Human Process*, Toronto, University of Toronto Press, 1971, pp. 341–356. Hogarth therefore develops a "phenomenological model" of sentencing focusing on how individual perspectives and attitudes influence sentencing decisions and how they affect the interpretation of fact patterns in cases. This is an alternative to the organizational model presented by Eisenstein and Jacob in *Felony Justice* and to the approach taken in this book. It was not adopted, however, because although officials in Detroit and Baltimore varied among themselves in the kinds of decisions they made, their choices were relative to the specific context within which they operated. If, for example, the officials had overlapped greatly in the proportion of recognizance bonds they granted, context and environment would be less important than the personal characteristics of the officials. The following table does not indicate this occurred.

Proportion of Defendants Granted Recognizance Releases by Officials in Detroit and Baltimore

Proportion of Defendants Granted Recognizance Release	Number of Officials[a]	
	Detroit	Baltimore
Below 10 percent	—	10
10–19 percent	—	9
20–29 percent	1	3
30–39 percent	6	1
40–49 percent	3	—
Over 50 percent	2	—
	12	23

[a] For Detroit the visiting judges and one Recorder's Court judge were excluded because of the small number of defendants arraigned by each of them. In Baltimore four commissioners were excluded for the same reason.

13. See, for example, the more elaborate analysis of a larger data set by Goldkamp, *Two Classes of Accused*, pp. 139–161. The results are not appreciably higher than those reported here.

2

Toward an Organization Theory Perspective of Felony Bail Processes

INTRODUCTION

Bail and pretrial release in America, it would seem, have been thoroughly explored. A recent bibliography, for instance, lists nearly 300 separate articles, reports, and books on the subject.[1] Yet, despite this attention, little theoretical movement has taken place. It is difficult to discern a reasonably coherent or systematic perspective that could be employed to explain the differences in the scope or severity of pretrial sanctioning that exist in local criminal courts.[2] In order to understand why Detroit and Baltimore had such divergent policies, then, it is necessary to take the first step toward creating such a perspective. In this chapter a conceptual framework resting on the "open social system paradigm" in organization theory is developed.[3] The basic building blocks used in constructing it are the environment and context of choice in criminal courts and the responses of court officials to the incentives and constraints emanating from them that shape pretrial release policies.

There are two major parts to the framework presented here. The first incorporates the contextual factors of uncertainty, risk, and resources that are held to influence the range of choice when court officials set bail and the environmental conditions associated with them. This contextual focus is then extended further to identify the modes of choice and ways in which pretrial release decisions are made. In other words, the framework highlights a set of factors affecting both what court officials or judges consider to be politically and organizationally feasible policies and the kinds of processes that emerge in courtrooms through which they typically make their decisions. After this part of the framework is introduced, the attention shifts to a basic process model of policy change, the second aspect of the framework. Changes in pretrial sanctioning are treated in this model as occurring when there are environmental disturbances prompting courts to assess the need for policy revisions. A pivotal feature of this model is the "risk minimization" rule that governs the court's search for and adoption of solutions that restore policy equilibrium.

CONTEXTS OF CHOICE: UNCERTAINTY, RISK, AND RESOURCES

Consider for a moment the problem court officials in large cities typically face when they make bail decisions. In all likelihood the defendants are strangers to them. They have no first-hand knowledge about their habits, backgrounds, or personal situations. The details of the alleged crime— the who, what, when, where, and especially why—are troublingly vague, if indeed they are known at all. Something about their past or more particularly their previous encounters with the law can be gleaned from their arrest record if they have one. A pretrial release investigator may have collected information about their current employment and marital status, other biographical data, and whether there is a family member or friend who will vouch for them if they are released. But again, some courts do not have pretrial release agencies or if they do the investigator may not have had time to interview some of the defendants or to verify the information. Defendants also may volunteer information about themselves in response to questioning, although their personal appearance, demeanor, and manner of addressing the court may prove more important as clues to what kinds of persons they are. Finally, other courtroom actors such as the prosecutor, defense counsel, or perhaps arresting officer may tell the court what they know or think about a defendant.

Based on this welter of information, discounted and weighed according to its reliability, the interests of its source, and relevance to the case at hand, court officials must decide a number of things. Is this particular defendant likely to appear in court? Is he or she dangerous and a threat to other citizens? What kind of bail decision is appropriate or just under the circumstances? If a cash bail seems necessary, how much should it be? Should it be an amount the defendant can post easily? But what if even a minimal cash bail means the defendant may spend some time in an already overcrowded jail? Would release on recognizance be preferable? But can the agency supervising their release guarantee their presence in court? On the other hand, if the defendant has a long criminal record or is accused of a serious crime, and shows signs of being dangerous, how large a bail will assure his detention while still not appearing excessive or unreasonable? And what does "reasonable" or "nonexcessive" mean under these circumstances? How will the community or certain groups react if the defendant unexpectedly regains his freedom? More particularly, how will they respond if he or she commits a crime while out on bail? Who will they hold responsible for this decision and its consequences?

Court officials, of course, do not ask and attempt to answer these questions for every case. The information at their disposal would be rarely adequate to provide the answers if they did. Hunches and habit as often as not fill the void, especially if time is short, there are other bail decisions to be made, and other court tasks need to be completed. Still the problem remains. How can officials be sure that even apparently routine and safe decisions will not backfire on them? Moreover, if the community rarely applauds and congratulates them for their successful release decisions, but pillories them when they make mistakes, what incentives do they have to take chances? Finally, and most difficult of all, how can they distinguish one from the other ahead of time?

These questions point to the major contextual characteristics affecting pretrial release decisions—uncertainty, risk, and resources. In the following sections each is discussed in more detail. Throughout, however, the importance of the court's political environment and the political function of pretrial release policies should be underscored. It is through these policies that benefits or penalties are allocated not just among citizens accused of crime—whose freedom is at stake—but to a host of other individuals, groups, and organizations in a city. Perceiving some gain or loss in material benefits or symbolic gratification from these policies, they are often willing to employ whatever political resources they have to retain or change them.

As a result, judges and officials involved in bail decisions must make choices, which by their nature are highly uncertain, in settings often fraught with risk. On the other hand, the feasibility of various choices depends on the legal, administrative, and detention resources which the political environment also provides the court. Accordingly, the scope and severity of pretrial release policies reflect the balance court officials struggle to create among these factors.

Uncertainty and the Perplexities of Choice

Criminal court processes, pervaded by uncertainty, are shaped by efforts to avoid it. Blumberg argued that bureaucratic due process arose because courts sought ways of "reducing the elements of chance in their work milieu."[4] Eisenstein and Jacob maintain that reducing uncertainty is a major goal of courtroom workgroups.[5] The point would not be grossly exaggerated, then, if Thompson's conclusion to his seminal *Organizations in Action* were paraphrased for present purposes to read, "Uncertainty appears as the fundamental problem for criminal courts and coping with uncertainty, the essence of its choice processes."[6]

Uncertainty is intrinsic to the task of making bail decisions. Officials

face the extraordinarily complex problem, at least in theory, of assessing the characters of criminal defendants so that bail options can be chosen that will reduce the likelihood of future undesirable outcomes. A major source of uncertainty is the lack of causal knowledge which Thompson referred to as "generalized uncertainty."[7] Ideally, decision makers ought to be able to determine with accuracy and confidence the probabilities and costs of various outcomes and then choose a means of minimizing or maximizing, as the case may be, the occurrence of the outcomes, again with considerable accuracy and a fair amount of confidence in the efficacy of the means.

This knowledge scarcely exists in criminal courts. As a result, defendants may be classified incorrectly as good or bad candidates for release and the wrong bail choice made. In other words, the problem of "false positives" and "false negatives" in sentencing decisions also plagues pretrial release choices.[8] Defendants who might be released safely are not, while those who perhaps should be incarcerated are freed. Even with the best of information and earnest effort, the opportunity for error generally can be expected to be quite high.[9]

Another kind of uncertainty (what Thompson termed "contingency uncertainty") occurs when the outcomes of organizational decisions are determined in whole or in part by the actions of others.[10] Except in the case of recognizance release and remands, the decisions of court officials do not effect directly their outcomes. The willingness or unwillingness of bondsmen to accept defendants who must post surety bonds for their release from custody is a prime and obvious example, leading one jurist to remark that bondsmen hold the keys to the jail in their pockets.[11] The ability of family members or friends to assist financially, or their willingness to act as "third parties" when a deposit bail must be made, also affect the outcomes of bail decisions. And, finally, instances have occurred when jail officials have refused to provide detained defendants with access to telephones so they can contact either their families or bondsmen to gain their release.[12] Whether judges or magistrates are aware of these problems and take them into account when they make their decisions is problematic.

The result, oftentimes, is that defendants may be freed or jailed, without the knowledge of the officials responsible for the decisions and contrary to the intent behind their choices, because of the actions or steps take by other persons. A somewhat extreme illustration of this problem, but only because of the drama and publicity surrounding it, was an incident involving a federal judge in Chicago who imposed bails of $500,000 for each of three defendants charged with an assassination attempt of a foreign ambassador, doubtlessly thinking bails of this size would detain them. To his astonishment and dismay, associates of the three posted the bails and after they were freed hijacked a plane with over 200 passengers at O'Hare Airport and forced the pilot to take them to Ireland.

A final source of uncertainty can be found in the conflicting goals of pretrial release. Bail is used not only to assure the appearance of defendants in court, along with the condition that it not be excessive, but also as a safeguard for the community and to protect victims or witnesses from harm. Other purposes include but are not limited to maintaining good relations with other courtroom participants or groups (not an insignificant goal at least for pretrial release directors who ranked it first in a recent study by the National Center for State Courts); eliminating the inequities of the bail system; and reducing overcrowding in the jail and the costs of incarceration.[13] The difficulty begins when there are multiple and conflicting goals that no single decision will satisfy simultaneously. Officials are then forced to decide the priority of the goals, usually with only a crude understanding at best of the tradeoffs involved in this exercise and perhaps only vaguely defined notions of their own values in the matter. Needless to say, the task becomes doubly complicated when the other kinds of uncertainty are taken into account.

Both objectively and subjectively the uncertainty enveloping bail decisions varies, although it is never wholly absent. In some instances the decision may seem clear. Defendants firmly anchored in the community with no previous arrests and charged with minor offences pose little difficulty as is also the case with defendants who are accused of heinous crimes after compiling lengthy lists of prior illegal activities. Between these extremes, much room remains for uncertainty. Experience on the bench, adherence to court custom regarding bail choice (specifically the 'bail tariff' discussed later), and routinization or reliance on a handful of simple decision cues all may help officials to cope with this problem; but it quickly should be added they are scarcely infallible guides.

Perceptions of uncertainty also are influenced by the quantity and quality of information court officials have about each defendant and equally as important information about the outcomes of earlier decisions. If this information is skimpy, unreliable, or unavailable, uncertainty is likely to be higher or exacerbated. It is relevant to note here that court officials depend on others for this information such as the clerk's office, prosecutors, police, pretrial release agencies, etc., for both task-related information and feedback about the results of their decisions. As a result, perceptions of uncertainty may be shaped and influenced by the methods and willingness of these organizations to collect, record, and distribute their information.

Risk and the Penalties of Choice

In 1974 a New York City judge, nicknamed "Turn 'Em Loose Bruce" by the Patrolman's Benevolent Association, was reassigned to civil court after a series of controversies stemming from his practice of setting low bail for defendants accused of violent crimes. He labeled his transfer as "banishment" and alleged in a lawsuit that the chief judge buckled under the pressure applied by the police union and two borough district attorneys. The judge made newspaper headlines once more in 1979 when he freed a man charged with attempted murder of a police officer decoy. The judge came under heavy criticism from the police and the mayor who defended his right to publicly criticize judges before the city's bar association. The judge's conduct also was examined by two judicial review commissions, one of which was responsible for deciding whether to recommend him for reappointment to the bench.

By itself uncertainty constitutes a serious difficulty for court officials. But, as this example suggests, the situation is aggravated for judges by the fact that they may be scolded, upbraided, or more severely sanctioned because actors in their environment dislike or are displeased with their decisions or their consequences. Suffet's argument that judges are encouraged to diffuse responsibility for their choices and consequently opt for conservative bail alternatives hinges on the influence exerted on judges by their sensitivity to public pressure and fear of the local media or newspapers if they make a mistake. According to one judge quoted by Suffet:

> If you let [the defendant] out on personal recognizance, with the understanding that he would reappear again for trial, and then the victim was badly injured, or killed, you have the problem of the newspapers coming in a very critical vein. You have to have some security for the particular judge.[14]

Judges can ill afford to ignore community expectations and the reactions of important groups or organizations; as the "final" decision maker judges are the "most vulnerable target of criticism."[15] The risk attached to their decisions involves two elements: the threat or actual imposition of negative sanctions, and, as the judge quoted above suggests, how much "security" or protection their official position affords them from sanctions. The critical effect of risk is that it determines the boundaries of political feasibility of various choices and of pretrial release policies more generally. Eisenstein argues that the existence and scope of discretion for officials depends on their ability to "choose between significant alternatives without incurring severe sanctions for picking one over the other."[16] This is a useful reminder that, even though the discretion of judges in setting bail is depicted generally as being very broad, some bail options may carry prices that discourage their use.

Two things should be noted about risk as a contextual characteristic at this point. First, while Suffet seemed to emphasize that public pressures usually push for more stringent, restrictive, or costly bail policies, there frequently are countervailing or at least opposing demands from groups for more lenient policies. The result is that court officials often are caught in the middle. A second important facet about risk for court officials is that their audience in the city, the actors in their political environment, respond just as vigorously to their decisions as to their consequences. The New York City judge mentioned earlier, for instance, was censured for his decisions, not because the defendants he released failed to appear in court or committed additional crimes while out on bail. Therefore, whatever their results, and frequently despite them, bail decisions *per se* carry considerable symbolic weight and may become the focus of conflict in the city.

Threat as one element of risk reflects, of course, the willingness and effort of environmental actors to inflict negative sanctions on court officials or to deny them various rewards. Obviously, the success of such attempts depends on the relative strength of the actors and their access to the courts. It also depends upon whether judges perceive that they are likely to succeed in these efforts. These perceptions supply important cues for court officials with the result that both the anticipation of sanctions and their imposition influence what they feel are feasible bail choices. It would be a mistake, however, to assume from this that officials invariably know ahead of time when some group or organization will object to their practices and whether they will succeed or fail in applying pressure. At best they must rely on what has happened in the past and look at current conditions to gain an idea as to possible reactions to decisions. The result is that threat itself has an uncertain quality about it.

The effects of threat, however, can be mitigated or aggravated according to the extent to which court officials are vulnerable to sanctioning, the second aspect or element of risk. Bail practices follow the political temperament of a city more or less closely depending on whether the positions of court officials make them susceptible to the imposition of penalties. For example, if judges receive little esteem in the city, their place in the court hierarchy is low, or their tenure is insecure, they face strong inducements to follow bail practices that least expose them to the threats of sanctions. One way of achieving this end is to reduce the visibility of decisions to outside actors by adhering to established bail practices, since they are likely to be a reflection of the court's previous efforts to cope with and adapt to its political environment.

Risk, then, primarily varies according to the political milieu of the court and with its institutional characteristics as they pertain to the security or vulnerability of its officials. Perceptions of risk, in addition, may reflect the composition of the court's docket or more specifically the seriousness of cases and charges making up the court's workload. Misdemeanors are unlikely to raise as many qualms as felonies, and minor felonies are less likely to provoke the anxiety and misgivings associated with major felonies. An organizational implication of this is that perceptions of risk are likely to vary across courts, depending upon the characteristics of crimes comprising their bail dockets.

Resources and Means of Choice

Uncertainty and risk create contextual incentives and disincentives that mold what court officials feel are feasible or permissible choices. Bail options such as recognizance release routinely may be dismissed as impractical or unreasonable for various crimes or, perhaps, for most if not all felonies. In some cities otherwise sweeping bail reforms stop short of drastically reducing normal bail amounts for fear of arousing political opposition.[17] However, pretrial release policies also depend on and are shaped by the configuration of resources—legal, administrative, institutional—to which courts have access.

State constitutions, statutory law, and higher court rulings permit courts to deny bail to criminal defendants, to impose financial and nonfinancial conditions as prerequisites for release from custody, to employ security or deposit bail in lieu of sureties, and on occasion to hedge the exercise of this authority through guidelines, although formal judicial discretion invariably remains broad. Pretrial release agencies, responsible for gathering information about defendants and supervising them when they are freed on recognizance, represent administrative resources for courts and can facilitate wider usage of nonfinancial forms of pretrial release. Important as these resources are, and in the case of legal authority fundamental to the operation of pretrial processes, the critical resource at the local level, often dictating how the other resources are employed, is the jail and its detention capacity.

Jails are the crucial underpinnings of local pretrial policies because, to put it starkly, without them pretrial sanctioning would stop. Remands obviously would be impossible if there were no place to detain defendants. Cash bails, regardless of their type or amount, only work when defendants know they will be jailed if they fail to post them. Even recognizance and other forms of conditional release ultimately rely on the threat of incarceration to enforce stipulations governing pretrial freedom. Jails, of course, do exist, and in the literature there are references to their role in pretrial decision making. Blumberg noted that "at times" in New York City "bail practices become a function of the extent of crowding in the short-term prison" used to house pretrial detainees, and Schaeffer subsequently provided empirical substantiation for this assertion.[18] Roth and Wice repeated the finding in Washington, D.C., and Wiseman found a similar situation in Seattle's "drunk court."[19] In each city bail practices became more lenient, particularly in regard to the use of recognizance, as the jails became overcrowded or threatened to exceed their capacity.

Jails, then, make pretrial sanctioning feasible while simultaneously limiting or constraining its scope and severity. It follows from this that pretrial release policies may vary across jurisdictions as direct reflections of the detention capacities of local jails. Larger jails relative to the volume of defendants will permit courts to pursue or retain more restrictive policies than if the jails were smaller. This obvious relationship, however, obscures a complex, somewhat subtle, interaction between jails and courts, especially when viewed over time. As the preceding references to overcrowding suggest, the detention capacity of jails can be rather elastic, and this elasticity provides courts with a form of "organizational slack." In *A Behavioral Theory of the Firm*, Cyert and March point out that slack absorbs "a substantial share of the potential variability" in an organization's environment and because of this "plays a stabilizing and adaptive role" in its behavior.[20] For courts, the existence of slack means that they can balance conflicting demands or adjust to new ones without severely jeopardizing their bases of political support.

Overcrowding, if it is tolerated by the community, is one important source of detention slack, allowing courts to respond to such events as sudden increases in caseloads, or perhaps seasonal variations, without altering their bail practices. It is not the only kind, however. Even within the constraints of the jail's official capacity, there are other sources of slack which if exploited can be used to increase the effective pretrial detention capabilities of the jail. The jail's detention function, for example, can be made "purer" by limiting or reducing drastically the incarceration of convicted minor offenders thereby making room for defendants awaiting disposition. Similarly, its function can be narrowed further to that of a pretrial felony detention center if most persons accused of misdemeanor or traffic offences are freed on their own recognizance or easily made cash bails. If other courts or law enforcement agencies also use the jail but can be persuaded to seek alternatives, their actions will create slack in the jail for a particular court. In other words, the prior function of the jail and whether it is shared by more than one court provide potential policy options, which, if taken, can free up detention slack and opportunities for a court to jail more felony defendants than it had previously.

Overcrowding, whether the jail's function is specialized or not, and whether more than one court uses the jail are three sources of potential slack. A final, and critical, source can be found in the population dynamics, or turnover, of jails. More time will be spent discussing this last source of slack since it will clarify how court policies can be key determinants in stabilizing or effecting changes in the detention capabilities of jails. It also will lay a basis for the process model introduced later in this chapter.

The turnover rate bears a simple relationship to a jail's capacity. Increases in the rate over a given period of time make room for additional prisoners while declines limit it or produce decreases. This means that jails with similar design capacities could have different detention capabilities if one has a higher turnover rate than the other. Jail populations vary with fluctuations on the balance between the inflow and outflow of prisoners. When the number of new prisoners entering the jail on a daily basis exceeds the number of prisoners leaving it, then, if over time this imbalance persists, the inmate population will grow. When the influx of new prisoners is less than outflow, the jail population will begin to drop. The volume of each of these streams of defendants is determined by different but not unrelated factors.

The number of defendants jailed on a daily basis reflects the stringency and cost of bail decisions made in court and the size and composition of its bail docket, i.e., the number of defendants arraigned daily and the seriousness of the charges lodged against them. If the characteristics of the bail docket remain the same but bail decisions for any reason become more strict, the influx of defendants into the jail will grow. By the same token, this influx will increase if the number of arraigned defendants mounts, but customary bail practices fail to change to prevent this increase from raising the jail population. Even when both of these factors do not change, more defendants will be incarcerated if the charges lodged against them for whatever reason become more serious since the frequency and size of cash bails imposed by courts generally are related directly to the severity of offenses. As a result, an increasing proportion and number of defendants probably will fail to make bail quickly enough to avoid detention. Over time, then, jail populations vary with the daily inflow of prisoners and the reasons for this variation may be due to any one of these three factors or to some combination of them.

The jail's outflow of prisoners, the counterbalancing force in this population equation, depends on the ability of inmates to post bail, the business rules followed by bondsmen regarding whom to accept as customers and when to demand collateral, and finally the policies of the court affecting the priority and speed with which it disposes of its caseloads and when it reviews the bails of detained defendants. If the economic circumstances of defendants change over time, but bails are set without regard to them or remain constant, improvements or declines in these circumstances will lead to corresponding rises or falls in the number of defendants capable of purchasing their pretrial liberty.[21] If bondsmen grow more cautious, becoming either more reluctant to post bail for certain defendants or less hesitant to demand collateral, the release rate for defendants will fall. Jail populations and the time defendants spend behind bars also fluctuate with the disposition process of courts; rising when they are too slow or inefficient to offset the influx of new jail prisoners and dropping when they are quick enough to create an outflow of prisoners greater than inflow.

A number of factors, then, have a bearing on the size and stability of a jail population. Some fall within the control of the court, others lie beyond its grasp. In addition, each may change independently of the other. An important consequence of this interplay among the factors affecting turnover is that fluctuations in jail populations may not be immediately deciphered by courts. The regularity of communications between the courts and jail authorities and the sophistication of the information collected about incarcerated prisoners and court dockets play key roles in identifying the causes of upswings, for example, and whether they are interpreted as permanent or merely transitory phenomena.

The major segments of this discussion now can be brought together to depict how sources of slack detention resources are linked to the characteristics of jail populations and their determinants. Figure 2.1 portrays these relationships. Slack resources can be generated by different policy options depending on the nature of the jail population. These characteristics in turn reflect the policies of the court and the actions or practices of other actors, such as bondsmen, affecting the inflow and outflow of jail prisoners. The options that emerge and that are available to the court are not necessarily mutually exclusive of one another; they may be combined or used separately depending on political conditions and the problems confronting the court.

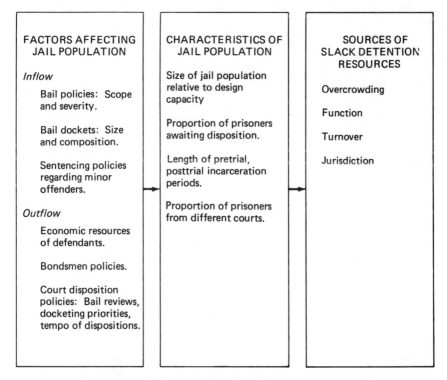

FIGURE 2.1   A Sub-Model of Organizational Slack in Pretrial Detention Resources.

MECHANISMS OF CHOICE: BAIL TARIFFS AND DECISION MODES

How are bail decisions made? What sort of decision process do court officials typically use? What kind of guides do they follow when making these decisions? The preceding discussion provides some clues to the answer for the last question. The contextual features of pretrial release decision making establish conditions under which court officials determine what they feel are feasible choices. This determination is both learned by them through trial, error, and a fair amount of tribulation, and taught to them by others with the result that they develop "bail tariffs" to help them decide. The ways through which bail decisions are made reflect a somewhat different set of contextual variables. Two have been mentioned several times already and include the size and composition of the bail or arraignment docket and the quantity and quality of information. To this list are added the accessibility of court officials during bail hearings to other actors and the conduct and demeanor of defendants.

Bail tariffs and modes of choice make up the basic behavioral components of the day-to-day process of making pretrial release decisions. This twofold characterization parallels Mohr's suggestion that a decision-making process is composed of a choice mechanism that includes both a "criterion for selecting the levels at which the various goals relevant to a collective decision will be satisfied" and "instrumental decision behavior."[22] His general hypothesis that "the operative mode of choice, or decision making, is determined by the specific conditions under which the decision is made" forms the basis for the second part of this discussion. The first part develops the notion of bail tariffs in more detail before turning to the modes of choice.

Bail Tariffs and Simplifying Choice

Bail schedules, lists of charges with specific dollar amounts itemized for each offense, were once common fixtures in American courtrooms. With the aid of these schedules, courts were able to expedite bail matters without a lot of procedural fuss and every defendant accused of the same crime got the same bail regardless of their personal circumstances. Reformers appalled at the use of the schedules sought to rid courts of them.

Bail schedules are examples of bail tariffs, differing only in their explicitness and formality, but serving the same function—simplifying the problem of setting bail. In this respect they illustrate the general organizational phenomenon in which organizations grapple with the problems of complexity and uncertainty by developing standard operating procedures, rules, and programs. Bail tariffs evolve through repetition for, as

March and Simon hypothesize, "When a stimulus is of a kind that has been experienced repeatedly in the past, the response will ordinarily be highly routinized."[23] On the bench only a short while, a judge's comments that bail decisions were getting easier with time illustrate this point. "I now know more what I am doing," he said, "I don't think as long. I look for those factors I think are important and decide."[24] After performing the bail task many times court officials come to rely on precedent and on the cues and guidelines previously used in similar kinds of cases. These "rules of thumb" define in effect what they believe are normal bails for normal kinds of offenses or situations.[25]

In many respects analogous to the "going rates" that structure plea bargaining, tariffs also shape the nature of the decision process. It is rare that bail decisions are produced through processes approaching rational models of choice in which decisions are the result of gathering complete information, drawing certain conclusions about the consequences of different options based on this information, and then selecting the appropriate form or amount of bail according to maximizing choice criteria. Rather, it is likely that the process involves a search by officials to establish whether or not they should follow custom. Setting bails and making pretrial release decisions, consequently, resemble a process of deciding if marginal, but sometimes not so marginal, revisions in the repertory of choices making up the bail tariff are necessary.[26]

Communication among officials and their socialization perpetuate tariffs. They learn about the bail decisions of their peers through personal conversations and by talking with other participants in the criminal disposition process. Knowledge about their pretrial release predilections also comes from reviewing the files, court records, and other documents handled in the course of their work. In addition, new officials usually have performed other roles or held other positions in the criminal justice system and know about the court's bail practices before being appointed or elected to the bench. This knowledge is an important aid when making their own decisions for the first time.

Tariffs, however, are not static. Nor is their content, the array of choices and prices for pretrial freedom, determined only by the personal views of court officials. Over time tariffs reflect an accumulation of adjustments by court officials to environmentally induced changes. Periodic jail crises or demands from influential actors in the city can effect alterations in resources or impose new constraints on courts that make previous options no longer feasible, institutionally or politically. State laws governing the kinds of bail a court may choose also may change. A major result of common environmental factors and of communication and socialization on the bench is the evolution of a court-wide bail tariff encompassing individual differences but reflecting the limiting effects on the court's particular history and political context.

Decision Modes and the Technology of Choice

Bail tariffs guide the deliberation of court officials, but they do not mechanically determine how they will be made. The ways courts manufacture decisions are described by Eisenstein and Jacob in terms of "work techniques" or the procedures used by courts to manipulate and transform certain resources, primarily information and authority, into decisions. They identify three major techniques—unilateral decision making, adversarial proceedings, and negotiations—as common to the criminal disposition process. They also argue that despite the fact that judges, prosecutors, and defense attorneys have the authority to "make unilateral decisions that eventually turn into dispositions" their "extensive" interdependencies with one another preclude them from exercising this authority with the result that unilateral decisions "play a minor role in the courtroom's work."[27] For at least two reasons, there is cause to expect that, unlike the disposition process, unilateral decisions figure more prominently in the bail-setting process.

Initial bail decisions, those made at the time of arraignment or shortly afterwards, do not require the collective efforts of the normal courtroom coterie of judge, prosecutor, and defense attorney. Only a judge or magistrate is needed to conduct bail hearings in contrast to preliminary hearings, pretrial motions, and certainly trials. Almost by definition, then, but depending ultimately on specific court rules and policies, unilateral decision modes often are characteristic of bail hearings. Furthermore, even when all members of courtroom organizations are present, the process still may be one-sided with the judge fixing bail without discussing the matter with anyone. Suffet, for instance, found that nearly half the bail decisions he observed were done unilaterally by the judge. Neither the prosecutor nor defense attorney attempted to participate and the judge did not encourage it.[28]

If unilateral decisions are commonplace in bail hearings, they still are not universal. Nonunilateral modes or procedures also occur, for as Suffet also discovered, conflict in the guise of bail suggestions, proposals, counterproposals, and sometimes extended argument by prosecutors and defense attorneys were typical of the rest of the bail cases in his study. Bearing in mind this distinction between unilateral and nonunilateral decision modes, a moment's reflection quickly makes it self-evident that the less accessible court officials are to other actors, the greater the likelihood that the work technique will tend to be unilateral in nature. However, this is a necessary and not a sufficient condition because, as Suffet found, the presence of prosecutors and defense attorneys does not guarantee their participation. Still, accessibility is a key contextual variable affecting how decisions are likely to be made.

The preceding hints at a change in the way unilateral decision making will be viewed here. Eisenstein and Jacob treat it as just one of three work techniques. It will prove more useful here to consider it as a category of related decision modes. There is ample evidence of unilateral decision making in bail hearings, but in some places it is described as being highly routinized while in others it is a situationally oriented procedure. Certainly one of the most frequently heard complaints is that bail is decided by rote. The hearings are brief, lasting sometimes no more than half a minute. The proceedings are attenuated, often amounting to little more than pronunciamentos from the bench. But, bail decisions also may be subject to "situational justice."[29] Court officials, as in the routine mode, still dominate the proceedings but defendants play a larger role. Their demeanor and response to questions may be viewed by officials as indications of disrespectful or arrogant attitudes with the result that they are penalized with more stringent bails than if they had behaved with greater deference.

Honesty tests are frequent features of the situational mode and are related to the presumption of defendant guilt that Blumberg argued permeated the actions of criminal court officials.[30] If defendants usually are presumed guilty of something, their attempt to offer explanations or to persuade judges that they can be released safely will be received with skepticism. Since their freedom depends on the bail decision, officials also may presume they have strong incentives to misrepresent themselves, to shade the truth or simply lie, and this gives officials the opportunity to assess the character of defendants by asking them questions for which they already have answers. When encounters are structured in this way defendants are given the chance to impeach themselves. If they are evasive or lie, they confirm the official's suspicions and show that they cannot be trusted or that they do not deserve a normal bail. As a judge in Detriot explained to Luskin:

> If he lies, the bail goes up . . . . I ask [the defendant] 'have you ever been arrested anywhere in the world before since the moment you were born?' What could be clearer? They try to weasle saying, 'I didn't know you meant traffic too' or 'I didn't know you meant juvenile.'[31]

In the situational mode court officials question defendants and use the response in making their bail decisions.

Under what conditions are these two modes of unilateral decision making most likely to occur? Two basic factors come to mind. The first pertains to the nature of the bail dockets, in particular, their composition and size. Eisenstein and Jacob hypothesize that the procedures used by courtroom workgroups in the disposition of cases become more routinized with the specialization of the workload and conversely cases are less routinely handled when they are diverse.[32] The size of the docket or volume of case handled during a single session of court or a given time period also affects routinization. As caseloads become heavier the procedures used by officials will be more streamlined in order to minimize inefficiency. The second factor is the quantity and quality of information officials have about defendants. Reliable information facilitates an expeditious handling of cases. Officials can set bail quickly with a feeling of confidence that there is less need to probe defendants with questions. When information is scanty and not especially dependable, officials must fall back on their ability to decipher the character of defendants from the way they behave before the bench.

Based on these two factors, bail decisions are more often made through the routine mode when the bail docket is large, comprised of roughly similar kinds of charges (all misdemeanors or all felonies, for example), and officials have most of the information they need and they can depend on it. The opposite set of conditions fosters the situational mode. Incomplete and unreliable information exacerbates the problem of uncertainty and forces officials to search for clues in the defendant's behavior to make their decisions. A light docket permits them to expend the time needed for this exploration. A mixed docket, made up of both misdemeanor and felony cases, under these circumstances heightens the perceived gravity of felonies, since they are usually less frequent, and against a background of minor crimes their seriousness and potential risk stand out for officials. As a result, they attract more attention from officials than misdemeanors, are assessed more carefully, and the choice of bail approached with greater caution.

Nonunilateral modes, such as adversarial proceedings and negotiations, as pointed out earlier, depend fundamentally on the accessibility of court officials to other actors. Dockets and information are relatively unimportant, although they may play a part in structuring the nature of the process or the frequency of conflict among participants. The location of bail hearings, when they are conducted, and court rules can aid or hinder the access of different actors to the officials and create biased patterns of participation normally not found at succeeding stages in the disposition process. The potential for influence that comes with access, however, depends on the nature of the relationship between these actors and officials. In negotiations, for example, Eisenstein and Jacob state that "much depends on the long-run relationships" between participants because of the importance of trust, empathy, and mutual understanding in lubricating the process.[33] These considerations are less critical in adversarial proceedings.

Table 2.1 highlights the contextual factors and their relationships with the decision modes that have been discussed. The underlying premise is that it is both necessary and desirable to recognize that more than one mode of decision making exists in pretrial release processes and that this variation can be explained largely by variation in context. Thus, when different courts are compared, the relative frequency of these decision modes will vary according to the contextual factors illustrated in this table. Courts with "pure" bail dockets, where bail hearings involve only

TABLE 2.1   Bail Decision Modes and Contextual Factors

	Bail Decision Mode		
	Unilateral		**Nonunilateral**
Contextual Factor	**Routine**	**Situational**	**Negotiation or Adversarial**
Access to official	Lower	Lower	Higher
Bail docket	Higher volume, pure docket	Less volume, mixed docket	Either
Quality of information	More complete, reliable	Less complete, unreliable	Either
Defendant behavior	Important	Very important	Less important

misdemeanor or felony defendants and officials conduct a large number of hearings within a given period, will tend to rely on routine decision modes although not exclusively. The expeditiousness with which these cases are processed will be furthered when officials have relatively complete and reliable information. The situational mode tends to be used in courts where officials have more time for each bail decision, there is a mixed bail docket, and if they often have poor information at their disposal during the hearings. Adversarial or negotiating modes will predominate under either docket or information conditions as long as other actors are present.

A FRAMEWORK FOR ANALYZING PRETRIAL RELEASE POLICIES

The basic elements employed in this study of pretrial release policies have been introduced. At this point these elements and their relationships are shown graphically as a way of summarizing the preceding discussion. Figure 2.2 builds upon a model of organizational choice behavior outlined by Mohr but adapts it to include factors pertinent to bail and pretrial release.[34]

The contexts of choice behavior discussed here are conceived as varied and complex reflections of the intrinsic nature of pretrial release decision making, the court's political environment, the policies pursued by the police and prosecutor's office, and the structure and rules of the court itself. Mechanisms of choice, the means through which decisions are made and guided in turn are shaped by the character of these choice contexts. Bail tariffs emerge as court-wide manifestations of ongoing and earlier efforts to cope with the problems of uncertainty, risk, and resources, while the mode of choice employed by the court depends on the patterns of access courthouse actors have to officials, the court's docket

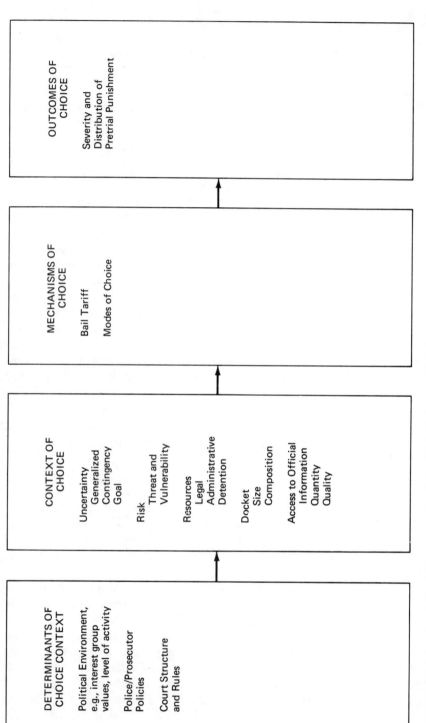

FIGURE 2.2 An Analytical Framework of Pretrial Release Policies.

characteristics, and the informational resources available to officials when making bail decisions. Through the operation of these mechanisms policy outputs and outcomes are produced that differ from one court to another in terms of frequency with which defendants are forced to post bail, the cost of these bails, and the rate at which defendants fail to regain their liberty.

The major function of this framework is to help organize the case study material which in turn will show its value and utility. Another equally important purpose, is that the framework also provides grounds for developing a *process theory* of policy change.

AN ORGANIZATIONAL CHOICE MODEL OF POLICY CHANGE

Environmental influences, conceived as playing a major role in shaping the scope and severity of pretrial policies, also play a crucial part in prompting changes in these policies. The court's functional relationships with the police, prosecutor, jail, bondsmen, and pretrial release agency make it vulnerable to policy changes by these organizations, and its political links and dependencies expose it and its officials to the imposition of negative sanctions. A central assumption is that like other organizations courts seek to control their environments through their policies or at a minimum adopt practices that will buffer them from adverse environmental pressures.[35] An important aspect of this assumption is that these efforts have equilibrating tendencies and that policy changes take place primarily when an existing equilibrium becomes unsettled. A basic model of policy change, drawn from the work of March and Simon and of Cyert and March, that incorporates this perspective is illustrated in Figure 2.3.

Courts, according to this model, adopt bail practices and case disposition policies, particularly those affecting the priority and speed with which cases are handled, that will achieve a balance between environmental risks and available resources. As long as these constraints are satisfied, the scope and severity of pretrial punishment will remain relatively stable from one time to the next. This situation can be upset for many reasons including rioting in the jail; newspaper exposés about jail conditions; public alarms over crime, or conversely, complaints that bail practices are too severe or court delays too long; revisions in state laws or rules affecting pretrial release; or changes in the behavior of bondsmen.

Regardless of the specific cause behind the disequilibrium, the search process for solutions tends to be narrowly focused, concentrates only on alternatives closely related to the problem, and employs satisficing rather than maximizing criteria when choosing an alternative. As a result, policy changes tend to be marginal in most instances. The major decision rule guiding this process is "minimize risk;" a rule closely related to the

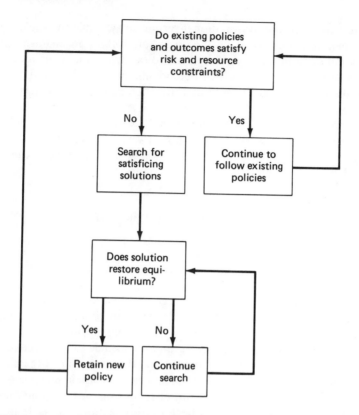

FIGURE 2.3   An Organizational Choice Model of Policy Change.

"minimum regrets rule" in decision theory.[36] Policy options are chosen when they are perceived as least likely to increase the odds of adverse political reactions while simultaneously ameliorating the conditions that gave rise to the problem.

The effects of this rule are straightforward when there is a sudden shock to the court as when persons of some notoriety unexpectedly gain their release or a defendant out on bail commits a sensational crime. To avoid further misadventures, officials are likely to tighten up their bail decisions by giving recognizance releases less frequently and by boosting the size of their cash bails. Both the permanence and extent of this reaction, however, depend on the vulnerability of the officials to sanctions, the amount of publicity surrounding the incident, the concern expressed by influential actors, and the existing amount of detention slack needed to absorb the additional defendants who probably will fail to post the higher bails.

The rule's implications are less clear-cut and the process more complex when there is pressure on the court to somehow improve jail conditions and reduce overcrowding, or if it feels the need to meet the demands of groups seeking more liberal pretrial release policies. Wholesale change would threaten the prevailing distribution of benefits, both substantive and symbolic, generated by current policies and inevitably heighten the risks involved. To avoid this eventuality, courts can accommodate these pressures and demands without revising their bail practices by drawing upon the slack commonly found in their disposition procedures.

Revision of these procedures are preferable to pretrial release reform for three reasons. First and most important, they generally produce less uncertainty and lower risks than bail reforms because there is wider political agreement on the importance of prosecuting defendants as quickly as possible than on what constitutes effective or fair bail policies. Second, many judges or magistrates may question the wisdom of freeing persons charged with crimes or possessing criminal records who normally would be detained or at least compelled to post substantial bail before their release. Under both of these circumstances, accelerating the pace of dispositions so defendants are detained for shorter periods, which relieves the jail of population pressures without increasing the number of freed defendants, becomes an attractive alternative to more sweeping bail policy changes. Finally, aside from the issue of risk, courts frequently lack the means of forcing obstinate members on the bench to follow new bail rules and, unless the need for change is clear and pressing, alternatives are pursued that will avoid the struggles needed to gain their cooperation.

Reform of pretrial release policies may be required when other efforts to reestablish equilibrium fail or current bail practices come under direct attack. Nevertheless, the reforms need not be dramatic since numerous changes can be made which satisfy the need to placate public demands. Pretrial release agencies, for example, may be created but the court may use recognizance release so stingily that the reform becomes merely symbolic. Another tack is to have the bails of detained defendants reviewed to determine if they were inadvertently refused recognizance release at arraignment or to see if their circumstances changed while in jail which might justify changing their bails. Such reviews, however, usually occur some time after the initial bail setting decision, which means defendants otherwise eligible for recognizance may already have purchased their release. Since they also involve second guessing the judgment of colleagues who set the bails, officials may be reluctant to change them frequently.

When circumstances demand more than marginal changes, courts still can temporize by either tinkering with the size of their bails or if state or local rules permit by using security bails more frequently. The appearance and, to a degree, the substance of reform are obtained, but defendants still must pay for their release. Consequently, the court does not appear as liberal as if it greatly expanded the use of recognizance release. Moreover, court officials may be spared political retribution for this move since security bonds reduce the role of bondsmen and this generally draws considerable support from the legal community and reform groups.

The choice process selects and tests policy alternatives, then, according to the risk avoidance rule, and if a policy change restores equilibrium the process comes to a halt. If it does not, the cycle of search and adoption resumes, using the same rule, until a balance is struck. The nature of the environmental shock disrupting the status quo, and the court's perception of its strength and the consequences of ignoring it, affect the likelihood of change and its extent. Equally important are the kinds and amounts of slack existing in the pretrial process as a whole. The relationship between detention resources and the factors affecting the inflow and outflow of prisoners structure the array of choices open to a court when grappling with disequilibrium and therefore the kind of changes it adopts when reacting to environmental disturbances.

A SUMMARY AND LOOK AHEAD

This chapter developed a theoretical framework and a model of policy change to analyze bail decisions in criminal courts. To accomplish this task, certain basic notions and concepts were drawn from current theories about organizational behavior. These theories greatly emphasize the role of an organization's environment and its efforts to control it or insulate itself from its effects; this emphasis were adopted here. From the literature on organization decision making and choice, the framework incorporated the concepts of uncertainty, risk, and slack resources, and the general perspective that courts behave like satisficing organizations in that they conduct limited searches for solutions to problems. The perspective that emerges here rests on the assumption that the decisional behavior of courts has equilibrating tendencies, and that changes in policies reflect efforts to reestablish equilibrium in accordance with the risk avoidance rule after the previous equilibrium has been disturbed by changes in environmental factors.

With the completion of the theoretical spadework in this chapter, the ground has been prepared for the analysis of Detroit and Baltimore in the next three chapters. The case studies are organized in accordance with the conceptual framework that has just been introduced. Chapter 3, focusing on Detroit, highlights in particular the centrality of detention resources in pretrial sanctioning, but it also goes a step beyond this by developing in greater detail the conditions and sequence of steps involved in pretrial policy change. The simple model of policy change in this chapter, then, is more fully explicated to create a process model depicting the conditions and sequence of steps taken by a court when it is faced with the need to make policy revisions. Chapter 4, on Baltimore, besides showing the difficulties of implementing the bail reforms introduced into the city's lower courts when they were reorganized, also provides an illustration of how and why a series of events surrounding the city jail failed to produce the same kind of response as in Detroit.

Chapter 5 turns to an investigation of the outcomes for felony defendants of the pretrial policies of these two courts and their severity, i.e., time spent in jail and income losses suffered by defendants. Of special interest in this chapter will be an analysis of the "political economy of surety markets" and how they affect the release rates of felony defendants who must post surety bonds for their pretrial freedom. An important conclusion of this analysis will be that the commonly accepted dictum that bondsmen hold the keys to the jail is false. Instead court policies determine the "efficiency" of bond markets by shaping the risks and resources of bondsmen and hence the opportunity for felony defendants to purchase their pretrial liberty.

REFERENCES

1. See the list of publications in National Center for State Courts, *An Evaluation of Policy Related Research on the Effectiveness of Pretrial Release Programs*, Denver, National Center for State Courts, 1975. This review of the literature also provides an excellent assessment of the "state of the art" although primarily from a methodological stance, and as its title states it focuses only on bail reform and not courtroom processes more generally.
2. In large part, the absence of comparative research has been a major stumbling block in developing a coherent theoretical perspective. For an early comparative effort that struggles to provide an institutional explanation, but ultimately fails, see Lee A. Silverstein, "Bail in the State Courts—A Field Study and Report," *Minnesota Law Review* 50 (March 1966): 621–52. Local conditions and environments were factors in Wice's sweeping survey of bail reform but the discussion tends to be conceptually limited and often times *ad hoc* in nature; more importantly the center of attention is fixed on pretrial release agencies and their procedures rather than on the courts. See Paul B. Wice, *Freedom for Sale*, Lexington, Mass., Lexington Books, 1974.
3. See Karlene H. Roberts, Charles L. Hulin, and Denise M. Rousseau, *Developing an Interdisciplinary Science of Organizations*, San Francisco, Jossey-Bass Publishers, 1978 for a useful review of the state of organization theory; and Lawrence B. Mohr, "The Frustration of Theory in Organizational Behavior," paper presented at the Annual Meeting of the American Political Science Association, New York, N.Y., 1978 for the problems in empirical research. For a current assessment of this conceptual approach to criminal courts, see Peter F. Nardulli, "Organizational Analyses of Criminal Courts: An Overview and Some Speculation," in Peter F. Nardulli (ed.), *The Study of Criminal Courts: Political Perspectives*, Cambridge, Ballinger Publishing Company, 1979.
4. Abraham S. Blumberg, *Criminal Justice*, Chicago, Quadrangle Books, 1970, p. 26.

5. James Eisenstein and Herbert Jacob, *Felony Justice*, Boston, Little, Brown and Company, 1976, pp. 27–28.
6. James D. Thompson, *Organizations in Action*, New York, McGraw-Hill Book Company, 1967, p. 159.
7. Ibid., pp. 159–60.
8. Norval Morris, *The Future of Imprisonment*, Chicago, University of Chicago Press, 1974; and Andrew von Hirsch, *Doing Justice*, New York, Hill and Wang, 1976.
9. On the problem of predicting "bail crime," see Arthur Angel, et al., "Preventive Detention: An Empirical Analysis," *Harvard Civil Rights—Civil Liberties Law Review* 6 (1971): 289–396. For the problems of predicting violence more generally see John Monahan and Lesley Cummings, "Social Policy Implications of the Inability to Predict Violence," *Journal of Social Issues* 31 (1975): 153–164. And regarding the validity of Vera-type measures used in making release decisions see Michael R. Gottfredson, "An Empirical Analysis of Pre-Trial Release Decisions," *Journal of Criminal Justice* 2 (1974): 287–303; and Michael B. Kirby, "Effectiveness of the Point Scale," Washington, D.C., Pre-Trial Service Resource Center, 1977.
10. Thompson, *Organizations in Action*, p. 159.
11. The jurist was U.S. Court of Appeals Judge Skelly Wright in *Ponnell v. United States*, 310 F.2d 698 (1963).
12. Ronald Goldfarb, *Jails*, Garden City, N.Y., Anchor Books, 1976; and Kenneth J. Lenihan, "Telephones and Raising Bail: Some Lessons in Evaluation Research," *Evaluation Quarterly* 1 (1977): 569–586.
13. National Center for State Courts, *Policymakers' Views Regarding Issues in the Operation and Evaluation of Pretrial Release and Diversion Programs*, Denver, National Center for State Courts, 1975. Note should also be taken of Lermack's discovery that prostitutes were encouraged to jump bail in Peoria, Illinois, so officials could reduce the costs of prosecution. The goals behind pretrial release policies often are considerably more diverse than ordinarily thought; see Paul Lermach, "Hookers, Judges, and Bail Forfeitures," *Administration and Society* 8 (1977): 459–468.
14. Frederick Suffet, "Bail Setting: A Study in Courtroom Interaction," in William B. Sanders and Howard C. Daudistel (eds.), *The Criminal Justice Process*, New York, Praeger Publishers, 1976, p. 222.
15. Ibid, p. 224.
16. James Eisenstein, *Politics and the Legal Process*, New York, Harper and Row, 1973, p. 217.
17. Roy B. Flemming, C. W. Kohfeld, and Thomas M. Uhlman, "The Limits of Bail Reform: A Quasi-Experimental Analysis," *Law and Society Review* 14 (Summer 1980): 947–976.
18. Blumberg, *Criminal Justice*, p. 59; and S. Andrew Schaeffer, *Bail and Parole Jumping in Manhattan in 1967*, New York, Vera Institute of Justice, 1970.
19. Jeffrey A. Roth and Paul B. Wice, *Pretrial Release and Misconduct in the District of Columbia*, Washington, D.C., Institute for Law and Social Research, 1980; and Jacqueline P. Wiseman, *Stations of the Lost: The Treatment of Skid Row Alcoholics*, Englewood Cliffs, N.J., Prentice-Hall, Inc., 1974.
20. Richard M. Cyert and James G. March, *A Behavioral Theory of the Firm*, Englewood Cliffs, N.J., Prentice-Hall, Inc., 1963, p. 38.

21. Improved economic conditions may explain why release rates rose between 1962 and 1971 since Thomas found that overall surety amounts for felony defendants in the cities he studied were quite similar for the two years. Wayne H. Thomas, Jr., *Bail Reform in America*, Berkeley, University of California Press, 1976, pp. 42–43.

22. Lawrence B. Mohr, "Organizations, Decisions, and Courts," *Law and Society Review* 10 (Summer 1976): 621–642.

23. James G. March and Herbert A. Simon, *Organizations*, New York, John Wiley and Sons, Inc., 1958, p. 140.

24. Mary Lee Muhlenkort Luskin, "Judging: The Effects of Experience on the Bench on Criminal Court Judges' Decisions," Ph.D. dissertation, Ann Arbor, The University of Michigan, 1978, p. 92.

25. Sudnow's notion of "normal crimes" provides the basis for these comments; see David Sudnow, "Normal Crimes: Sociological Features of the Penal Code in a Public Defender Office," in Richard Quinney (ed.), *Crime and Justice in Society*, Boston, Little, Brown and Company, 1969.

26. Since their approach differs from the one presented in this study, it is worth noting the work of Nagel and his associates in developing normative rational models of pretrial release decision making. See Stuart Nagel, Marian Neef, and Sarah Slavia Schranim, "Decision Theory and the Pre-Trial Release Decision in Criminal Cases,' *University of Miami Law Review* 31 (1977): 1433–1491; Stuart Nagel, Paul Wice, and Marian Neef, *Too Much or Too Little Policy: The Example of Pretrial Release*, Beverly Hills, Calif., Sage Publications, 1977; and Stuart Nagel, Marian Neef, and Paul Wice, "Determining an Optimum Percentage of Defendants to Release before Trial: Applying Inventory Modeling Concepts to Legal Policy Problems," *Journal of Criminal Justice* 6 (1978): 25–33.

27. Eisenstein and Jacob, *Felony Justice*, pp. 30–31.

28. Suffet, "Bail Setting," p. 215.

29. Maureen Mileski, "Courtroom Encounter: An Observation Study of a Lower Criminal Court," *Law and Society Review* 5 (1971): 471–538.

30. Blumberg, *Criminal Justice*, p. 69.

31. Luskin, "Judging," p. 85.

32. Eisenstein and Jacob, *Felony Justice*, p. 63.

33. Ibid, p. 33.

34. Mohr, "Organizations, Decisions, and Courts," p. 627.

35. Besides Thompson, *Organizations in Action*, see also Donald P. Warwick, *A Theory of Public Bureaucracy*, Cambridge, Harvard University Press, 1975.

36. Charles A. Lave and James G. March, *An Introduction to Models in the Social Sciences*, New York, Harper and Row, 1975.

3

Limited Resources and Policy Change: Felony Bail Processes in Detroit

INTRODUCTION

In the years following its massive racial riot in 1967 as violent crime and homicides reached unprecedented heights, Detroit, the car capital of America, its "motor city," won the dubious distinction of being relabeled by the national media as its crime capital and "murder city." Locally, the evening newspaper published daily tallies of crimes committed in the downtown area and surrounding inner-city neighborhoods, while the television stations drew their viewers' attention to the city's growing crime problem and seemingly endless stream of murders. It was scarcely surprising, then, that four years after the riot over 50 percent of Detroit's white residents and nearly 45 percent of its black citizens felt that crime was the city's most critical problem.[1]

If pretrial punishment simply reflected the public's concern over law and order as expressed in survey polls, Detroit's bail practices in 1972 surely would have been expected to be more stringent than they were. Instead Recorder's Court had adopted relatively nonpunitive policies, both in comparison to Baltimore and to other large cities, because of countervailing pressures applied by politically active groups.

However, it would be a mistake to think of Recorder's Court's reaction to this pressure in mechanical terms, as somehow automatic or preordained. Although there was a "logic" behind the court's moves as it tried to cope with the many conflicting demands placed on it—a logic based on minimizing the political risks associated with changing pretrial policies—the court's decisions were greatly influenced by external events over which it had little control, and, like the riot, were difficult to predict or foresee. But this is getting ahead of the story. To lay the basis for this analysis, it is necessary to start by considering the political context of Detroit's felony court and the ways in which its judges made bail decisions. Once this is done, attention can be turned to detailing the process of policy change in this city.

THE POLITICAL ENVIRONMENT OF BAIL IN DETROIT

"Conflict runs deep in Detroit," according to Banfield in his survey of the city's politics completed in the early 1960s before the 1967 civil disturbance.[2] If the city's politicians failed to maintain a delicate balance among its many "bitterly antagonistic interests," he speculated, the 'dynamite may go off." Frequently upsetting Detroit's precarious political balance and igniting these explosions were battles over law and order issues.

The mayor at the time of the riot, for example, had defeated unexpectedly the highly favored incumbent in 1961 when Detroit's large black community swung its support behind his candidacy because of its anger over the indiscriminant arrest of 1,500 black men the year before during a police dragnet for a murder suspect. During this decade and into the seventies prominent black citizens, including a judge, complained of police harassment and disrespect. In 1967, on the other hand, just three months before the riot burst out, irate white neighborhood associations mounted a recall campaign against the mayor accusing him of doing little about what they saw as a worsening crime problem during his terms in office. The riot, which occurred roughly 25 years after the last racial upheaval in 1941, began when police raided a "blind pig," or illegal drinking place, in the near west side ghetto. Before it subsided a week later, 44 persons had been killed, hundreds of others were injured, and over 6,000 people had been arrested and detained, some in buses, others in Detroit's cavernous convention hall, because the jail was filled.[3]

By 1974 the tangled issues of race, crime, and law enforcement reached a symbolic apogee when Detroit's first black mayor was elected after defeating the white police chief who retired from the department to run for the office. Throughout the campaign a major issue was whether a controversial plainclothes police unit operating primarily in black neighborhoods would be continued under the new administration. On one side black leaders and liberal white groups accused the unit of killing over 20 persons and of using entrapment and unnecessary force when apprehending suspects. On the other side, it received strong support from white neighborhood groups, the Detroit Police Officers Association, and a popular television commentator.[4]

Race and crime, then, were intricately interwoven in Detroit politics. While this is generally true of most large American cities, the form and substance these issues take vary in part according to the extent to which blacks are mobilized around concerns over the role of the police and courts in their communities, the degree to which they have achieved political power, and whether there are white supporters for their concerns. In Detroit blacks clearly had been vocal in their criticism of the police, and after the riot they were joined by whites in criticizing the city's criminal court. Equally as important the black community had reached a position of considerable influence by the early 1970s.

Blacks made up 42 percent of Detroit's population in 1970 according to the Census; this proportion was undoubtedly higher by 1972. The black community was well organized; its local chapter of the NAACP for example was the largest in the country and blacks held prominent positions in the United Automobile Workers, the AFL-CIO, and in the labor movement's political action groups.[5] Black representation on city council failed to mirror the city's racial composition, however, because of the system of at-large elections (only two of the nine seats were held by blacks in 1972). But a black mayoral candidate in 1970 was defeated only narrowly by the white former sheriff, and, of course, as just mentioned, a black state senator won the mayoral office in 1974. On Recorder's Court, 5 of the 13 judges were black as were 3 of the 7 new judges who took their places on the bench after its expansion in 1973. A black court administrator was appointed in 1971 and a black held the position of Wayne County Sheriff.

At roughly the same time that blacks began to move into positions of political power a number of interracial groups, formed in the aftermath of the riot because of the "glaring injustices committed in the courts in 1967," as one group stated, were becoming increasingly active in their reform efforts. During the riot Recorder's Court judges, with the exception of one liberal black, agreed to the prosecutor's request that arrested persons receive bails ranging from $10,000 to $15,000. Little attention was paid to the actual nature of the offense, and judges even routinely barred defendants from having legal representation. Hostility toward defendants and suspension of normal legal procedures were explained by the fact that the judges were "filled with fear and doubts" as they watched smoke rising from fires burning throughout the city. As one stated at the time, "What we're trying to do here is keep them (rioters) off the streets." Afterward, another judge told the *Detroit Free Press* that, "We had no way of knowing whether there was a revolution in progress or whether the city was going to be burned down or what."[6]

After the riot the Interfaith Action Council, an association of area churches, formed the Equal Justice Council to assume a community organization and information role. An extensive court watching program was undertaken to determine the quality of treatment received by minority groups and low income defendants and a study of misdemeanor cases by a prominent University of Michigan sociologist was commissioned to provide empirical support for its position that justice was allocated unfairly according to the race and socioeconomic status of defendants.[7] Annual conferences were convened to publicize criminal justice problems, and pamphlets and leaflets were distributed to schools, civic organizations, block clubs, and churches. Its "Fact Sheet on Bail Bond" succinctly stated its views regarding bail: "The American Bail Bond System discriminates against and punishes poor people while releasing the rich." Of the four board members, one was an officer in the League of Women Voters and another was treasurer of the local chapter of the American Civil Liberties Union. In November of 1973 the council's executive director, a black female social worker, ran successfully for a seat on city council.

The Urban Alliance, like the Equal Justice Council, also was formed shortly after the riot. Describing itself as a "bi-racial, interfaith, nonpartisan" organization, it rated candidates for public office according to their views on such issues as full employment, police-community relations, law enforcement, and racial or ethnic discrimination.[8] To assure that its endorsements carried weight with candidates, the alliance sent voter guides to carefully selected areas of the city where it felt they would have the greatest electoral impact. Its executive committee and board of directors, comprised of nearly 100 members, included representatives from the UAW, AFL-CIO, New Detroit, Inc., Legal Aid and Defenders Association, the Wayne County Neighborhood Legal Services, the city's congressional delegation, major churches, the Guardians (a black police association), and a prominent black social group, the Cotillion Club. In 1972 the alliance rated two incumbent conservative judges running for reelection as "unacceptable" and supported their more liberal challengers.

A third group, Team for Justice, started in 1968 with financial support from the Catholic Archdiocese of Detroit. It concentrated on assisting and counseling prisoners in the Wayne County Jail and performing liaison work between the inmates, their families, attorneys, and probation officers. In 1972 it created Citizens for Pre-Trial Justice to pursue bail reform through litigation, legislation, and public information. An employee of Recorder's Court's Release on Recognizance Program participated openly and actively in the organization, providing it with information about release practices on the bench. It also was linked through its membership with the Interfaith Action Council and the recognizance program of Wayne County Circuit Court. In 1974 the group brought suit against Detroit's largest bonding agency for charging excessive bail fees.

Citizens for Pre-Trial Justice developed an elaborate set of standards and principles to evaluate bail policies and reform proposals. At both the state and local levels, it urged adoption of legislation or programs based on the presumption that defendants charged with noncapital offenses would be released on their own recognizance unless the prosecutor's office could show at the time of arraignment that there was some justification for more restrictive bails. Surety bonds, it argued, should be prohibited to eliminate bondsmen and the existing state provision for 10 percent security bonds in misdemeanor cases extended to include felony defendants. According to its program, incarcerated defendants would be entitled to periodic court reviews of their bail status and a speedy trial rule adopted by the state so felony cases would be completed within 90 days. Finally the group supported legislation that would provide detained defendants with financial compensation for the time spent in jail which would be applied toward the payment of fines in the same way that credit for time spent in jail was applied to prison sentences.

Important segments of Detroit's defense bar shared the prodefendant perspectives of these groups. The Legal Aid and Defenders Association, a private organization with 12 staff attorneys many of whom were black, adopted an aggressive adversarial posture in representing defendants assigned to it by Recorder's Court. This stance was based on the ideological belief that the police, prosecutors, and courts were biased against defendants and that "wide-spread and deep-seated racial prejudice shaped much of what happened" in Detroit's criminal justice system.[9] Public defenders were not alone in their beliefs, moreover, since a sizable number of private defense attorneys and noncriminal lawyers were equally as critical of conditions in Detroit and, most importantly, were willing to act on these beliefs.

On January 26, 1971 a group of attorneys representing inmates in the Wayne County Jail filed a civil complaint in the County Circuit Court against the sheriff, jail administrator, County Board of Commissioners, County Board of Auditors, and the director of the Michigan State Department of Corrections. The complaint demanded that the court "eliminate the depraved, inhumane, and barbaric conditions in jail including the filthy, sardine packed cells . . . ."[10] The attorneys in this case included a self-proclaimed Marxist (who later won election to Recorder's Court in 1972), private defense attorneys, and attorneys from the Wayne County Neighborhood Legal Services, the NAACP Legal Defense Fund, and the Detroit Chapter of the National Lawyers Guild. They asserted that the jail was overcrowded as a direct result of the surety bond system and on the first page of their brief squarely addressed this issue and its relation to the economic status of the prisoners.

> . . . [A]pproximately 1,100 persons . . . are incarcerated at the jail and deprived of their liberty solely because they, unlike wealthier persons accused of crime, cannot afford the price of bail . . . . [M]ore than 500 inmates are being held simply because they cannot afford the price of a $2,500 bail bond or less; more than 300 of such persons are being held simply because they cannot afford to post a bond of $1,000 or less.[11]

Because the jail was overcrowded three persons often shared the same cell which meant that one of them had to sleep on the floor near the open toilet.[12] In order to eliminate these conditions the attorneys argued that state and city housing standards applied to the jail and that it violated these standards by failing to allow at least 52 square feet per inmate in the cells. None of the cells in the jail's older section met this standard and those in the newer section, if the standards were followed, would house only one person at a time.

On March 24, 1972 circuit court ruled in favor of the plaintiffs and decreed among other things that by the end of the year the jail population had to be limited to 813 persons.[13] In the event this ruling was not followed and the population exceeded the limit, the sheriff would be held in contempt of court. The sheriff thus faced the Hobson's choice of refusing to detain defendants from Recorder's Court to avert overcrowding or risk being cited for contempt of court—either choice would provoke a crisis in the city's criminal justice system. As it happened, he did not have to make this decision since the jail's average daily population fell to about 660 prisoners, and went even lower toward the end of the year as Recorder's Court began to increase its use of recognizance release. The dynamics of this change will be discussed more thoroughly later in this chapter.

Detroit's media paid quite a lot of attention to crime in the city, but with the court case casting new light on the facility they began to shift their attention toward the jail, especially as various incidents within it furthered its newsworthiness. In February 1971 shortly after the complaint was filed, a man jailed for traffic violations hanged himself. A month later a 19-year-old inmate died of meningitis. During just the first two months of 1971 alone, 13 prisoners attempted suicide.[14] A locally produced television documentary entitled "The Cage" described various problems in the jail. In late 1972, two months before the jail's population limit went into effect, the *Detroit Free Press* filled its editorial page with interviews with the sheriff, a county commissioner, and an 18-year-old prisoner who had been homosexually raped in the jail.[15]

Overall, then, the political landscape of Recorder's Court at this time swirled with strong currents of prodefendant sentiment—currents, it should be noted, that were unimpeded by Detroit's loose political structure, which lacked strong political parties or ward-based machines and reflected the city's traditions of racial militancy, union activism, and political reform. The result was a political setting where groups seeking to change criminal justice policies formed easily and were able to operate freely.

Risk and Positional Vulnerability in Detroit

Political conditions surrounding pretrial release policies were shifting in Detroit during this time. The emergence of reform groups after 1967, the rise in prodefendant sentiment, and growth in black political effectiveness signaled that political changes were taking place. Still the cues emitted from the court's environment were mixed and conflicting, a reflection of the city's unsettled political condition. The jail case, the critical publicity that followed it, and challenges in the voting booth represented one set of cues. Another set came from the media's continuing attention to crime, white neighborhood associations, and public organizations, particularly the police. Interpreting these cues and weighing their consequences were important political problems for Detroit's judges in 1972.

Recorder's Court judges were elected officials whose public careers depended on their success in the voting booth. They could ill afford to be entirely impervious to the political consequences of their decisions or behavior on the bench. The following review of election results indicates the judges were relatively safe from defeat after gaining their positions on the court. Yet, this appearance to some extent is deceptive. Competition for these positions was often keen because of their attractiveness to candidates and because the city's relatively open recruitment process did not stifle challenges to sitting judges.[16]

Recorder's Court judges were paid over $30,000 a year in 1972 and their positions were equivalent to circuit court judgeships in Michigan. Adding further luster to the bench was the fact that it had been used successfully as a stepping stone to higher courts. Between 1968 and 1972 two of the four vacancies on the bench were created because one judge was elected to the Michigan Court of Appeals and another was appointed to Federal District Court. Thus, in 1972 when seven new positions on Recorder's Court were being filled, competition in the primaries was intense with 43 contenders vying for the 14 ballot slots in November general election. Recorder's Court judges were elected in nonpartisan elections for 6-year terms, but in some instances reached the bench by being appointed to fill a vacancy. Appointed judges had to run in the next regularly scheduled election in order to serve the rest of their unexpired terms, although the advantage of being an incumbent and having name identification reduced substantially their chances of defeat.

Between 1968 and 1972 none of the three appointed judges (two of whom were black) lost their election bids for the office. Two, in fact, faced no opposition at all, but a third (one of the appointed black judges) met considerable primary competition in 1968, a year after Detroit's devastating riot and one in which law and order was a major issue in local, state, and national politics. In the primary this judge found himself pitted against nine other contenders. It was a tight race. Out of the 137,035 primary votes, he received 22,386 or about 16 percent. A mere 552 ballots separated him from his second place competitor and the third place contender fell only 1,667 votes short of defeating the judge. In the general election, however, he handily defeated his challenger by over 30,000 votes, receiving 55 percent of the vote tally. When he ran for reelection in 1974, he was unopposed.

Nearly half of Recorder's Court was up for reelection in 1972 with 6 of the 13 judges campaigning for six-year terms. Two incumbents ran unopposed. The other 4 faced 6 primary challengers for the eight November election slots. The 4 incumbents experienced relatively little difficulty winning the primary and November elections. Despite the apparent ease with which they won their victories, the campaign was bitter and uncovered the racial, ideological, and economic fissures dividing Detroit. The 2 judges with conservative reputations received "unacceptable" ratings from the Urban Alliance, while gaining wholesale support from the white homeowner groups (one judge had been a founder of the Greater Detroit Homeowners' Council). Both major newspapers questioned their legal capabilities and refused to endorse them. The tenor of the election, in which one of the liberal incumbents actively campaigned against his conservative colleagues, is suggested by the following quote:

> [T]he election process reflected many of the basic divisions in the political life of the city . . . . According to a newspaper report, one candidate told a white homeowners group, 'It's them against us.' 'Them' included the UAW, superliberals, and those who wanted more black judges.[17]

The election did not settle which ideological view or group would dominate Detroit's court. The two conservative judges won their races, but ran 40,000 votes behind a black liberal who was top vote getter. The Marxist lawyer involved in the jail case was among the winners of the seven new court seats filled at this time, coming in second to a candidate with a popular Irish name and a veteran of 20 years on one of the city's civil courts. A female attorney from the Legal Aid and Defenders' Association also won a place on the bench. Three of the new judges were black; one of whom had been a prosecuting attorney for 17 years.

The diversity of views introduced into Recorder's Court through the city's recruitment process, it should be noted, could not be narrowed by the presiding judge. Elected by the judges for a year at a time and unable to serve consecutive terms, the position had little formal authority. Court assignments normally were rotated among the judges to handle the court's varied tasks and thus could not be used to sanction the recalcitrant. Whatever consensus the presiding judge forged on the bench depended on his personality and skills of persuasion.[18] Other than these informal processes, Recorder's Court judges were not susceptible to internal sanctions or penalties. "Visiting judges," however, were somewhat of an exception.

During 1972 40 of these judges spent varying lengths of time in Recorder's Court handling mostly preliminary examinations, but also arraignments and trials. Their positions differed from Recorder's Court judges. Temporarily assigned to the court to aid in processing its heavy caseload, visiting judges tended in bail matters to follow the lead of the presiding judge who boasted during an interview that when he became displeased with how a visiting judge performed he had him removed. In the opinion of one defense attorney, the visiting judges "learned fast" what Detroit's bail practices were. If they set higher than normal bails, lawyers talked to the presiding judge to get them reduced. After a while he "couldn't see much difference" between their bail decisions and those made by Recorder's Court judges.

In summary, then, on a day-to-day basis Detroit's regular judges held positions that gave them a high degree of autonomy and did not make them highly vulnerable to either internal or external negative sanctions. Still, their careers were at stake and this bound them to the constraints of their political environment and the possibility of electoral defeat.

Coping with Uncertainty

Uncertainty is an intractable problem when setting bail. Court officials must try to anticipate what defendants might do if released in order to protect the safety of the community, or at least not jeopardize it unnecessarily, and assure their appearance in court. At the same time, the bails should be fair in some sense to defendants and reasonably commensurate with their circumstances. Moreover, some consideration may have to be given to jail conditions. The tension between these and other goals is heightened by the inescapable fact that judges never know with certainty whether or when defendants will make bail or what they will do if they are released or detained.

After 18 months on the bench, a judge vividly recalled a time when he had been "jolted." At their arraignment before a different judge on rape charges, two defendants received cash bails of $50,000 and $70,000. The judge thought the amounts were excessive and, although he felt the charges were serious, agreed to a defense motion to reduce them. The reductions, he decided, would be symbolic so that while the bails were lower the defendants still would not be able to make them. He accordingly reduced the bails to $15,000 each. A short time later he discovered through the newspapers that one of the defendants posted bail and had been rearrested on a murder charge. "It was a real jolt," he said. "I'm sure that it affected me emotionally" and it probably influenced his later decisions, but "you try to keep it within certain bounds; you try to limit it."

Short of incarcerating every defendant, judges have few ways of eliminating this kind of uncertainty entirely or reducing it to a negligible level. One means of coping with the problem, however, was by "trusting the system." Because Detroit's judges were thoroughly familiar with the court's procedures, they either could rely on earlier decisions to absorb the uncertainty surrounding a decision or look to subsequent procedures to ratify or modify decisions about which they were unsure. For example, after finishing a bail hearing a judge, alluding to the prosecutors in the Warrant Section, remarked, "I expect they looked that one over pretty carefully. This being his first charge." Judges also frequently told defendants that their bails would be reviewed at their preliminary examinations. The purpose of these comments, of course, may have been to "cool out" defendants upset with the judge's decision, but it also suggests that judges viewed their decisions as conditional and that if they made a mistake it would be corrected later.[19]

In the following incident, the defendant, charged with armed robbery, was arraigned before a liberal black judge.

The judge tells the defendant he is charged with being armed with a blue steel revolver, that he put fear in the victim, and took a TV set and a wrist watch.

The defendant says that he can't pay for his own lawyer. "Why?" The defendant responds he was laid off and has just been called back. Replying to the judge's questions, the defendant tells the judge he is married and has five kids. "Ever been in any trouble before?" "I been incarcerated, sir." "Are you on parole now?" "No sir, I been off for two years." "Are you on probation now?" "No, sir."

The judge sets the bond at $5,000. The defendant then asks, "Could I talk a minute, your honor? I been frank about myself. I'm a probationary employee and I just got called back. I ain't got no money to get out and if I don't get out, I'm going to lose my job."

The judge then tells the defendant. "Look at your record. The charge is armed robbery. The examining magistrate is going to have to look at this. I can't let you walk out of here."

Since the defendant had a criminal record and apparently had served a prison term, this example may seem a bit extreme. The point gains further support in the next example where the defendant also was charged with armed robbery, but did not have a record. The defendant's mother and lawyer were present, an unusual occurrence in Detroit.

The attorney requested personal bond, adding he wouldn't belabor the purpose of bail to assure the appearance of defendant. He asked the judge to release the defendant on personal bond and place the defendant in the attorney's custody.

The lawyer argued the family would have difficulty raising funds for their son's defense and he would prefer to have the bond money used for this purpose. The judge responded the preliminary examination was on the ninth and that was only seven days in jail. They could go over the bail in more detail at that time.

Denying the request for personal bond the judge said, "I just can't. Not on this kind of charge. I just can't give a personal bond." Bond was set at $1,000.

In light of the fact that the median cash bail for armed robbery was $5,000 in Detroit, the amount imposed by the judge in the first example, bail was unusually low in this case. It apparently was a compromise between the attorney's explicit statement that his fee was at stake and a serious charge for which less than 5 percent of the sample defendants were granted personal bonds. The compromise's fairness was enhanced from the judge's view by the fact that the bail would be reviewed within a week after arraignment.

Comments by another judge provide a larger perspective of how successive steps in the disposition process helped judges cope with uncertainty. He described a case where the day after the preliminary examination, a defense attorney asked him as the trial judge assigned the case to consider a change in bail or a reduction in bond amount. Frequently, the judge explained, these motions were not formal; to expedite matters they often were informal talks. By moving this quickly, he pointed out, defendants could have as many as three different judges consider their bail in approximately a week's time since preliminary examinations were scheduled 7 to 10 days after arraignments. If a defendant failed to get his bail reduced after these reviews, there were probably good reasons why his bail was left unchanged. Moreover, if the original bail was abnormally high or "off the wall," according to this judge, the rapidity of Detroit's procedures meant that the defendant would spend only a week in jail, a consideration mentioned by the judge in the previous example.

Underlying this judge's comments was the view that Detroit's procedures increased the odds that defendants would be treated fairly. Persons who should have been released when they were arraigned but were not probably would be released at later stages after other judges had reviewed the bails. By "trusting the system" Detroit's judges reduced the uncertainty regarding the proper balance between defendants' rights and their personal circumstances and the possible threat they might pose to the safety of others. But coping with uncertainty in this manner may have biased the resolution of this conflict. By assuming their mistakes would be corrected at a subsequent stages, the judges implicitly increased the incentives to punish. Rather than taking a chance when the charge was serious or when there was a prior record, they could impose a cash bail believing that it would be reviewed later on with the consequence, however, that the defendant would be incarcerated in the interim, pay a bail price, or both.[20]

Still, no antidote for uncertainty is ever foolproof, as the following incident amply illustrates. Besides showing the effects of being "jolted," this incident suggests that another way of coping with this problem is by learning from past experiences, although the nature of this lesson may be broader in its effects than might be expected. In early November of 1972 an airplane was hijacked by three men to go to Cuba, two of whom had been released on surety bails after being arraigned on rape charges before the presiding judge. Immediately afterward his bails became much more stringent.

Before the hijacking, the proportion of personal bonds for a sample of 180 defendants arraigned before him had been 70 percent; afterward it fell to 41 percent for 139 cases.[21] The proportion of defendants receiving cash bails over $10,000 jumped from 6 percent to nearly 19 percent. What makes these changes particularly interesting is the fact that they were not confined to rape cases. The proportion of defendants accused of carrying concealed weapons who were freed on personal bonds went from 89 to 55 percent. For defendants with drug charges the proportion dropped from 84 to 62 percent. The most dramatic change in the judge's behavior took place when he set bails for defendants accused of burglary or of breaking and entering. Their chances of receiving personal bonds plummeted sharply from 86 percent before the hijacking to a mere 12 percent.

Uncertainty about the outcomes of decisions, the likelihood of "jolts," an unsettled political environment, and limited detention resources were crisscrossing pressures on the judges in Detroit. On the one hand, apprehension over the consequences of releasing felony defendants encouraged caution while on the other the means for detaining them were constrained. How, then, were decisions on a case-by-case, daily basis made in Recorder's Court? Were defendants closely scrutinized as they stood before the judges awaiting the decision affecting their release from custody? To what extent were bail hearings adversarial in nature? Or where these decisions routinized with pretrial liberty meted out quickly and hastily? The following section focuses on the answers to these questions.

ROUTINIZED DECISIONS DURING A TIME OF TURBULENCE

Typically, bail setting in Detroit was done through the routine decision-making mode.[22] Hearings were conducted quickly and involved few participants besides the judge, an "arraignment officer," and, of course, defendants. Honesty tests, however, were used sometimes by judges with the result that when defendants failed them the decision mode became situational. Bargaining was rare. Arraignments were held too soon after arrests for most defendants to retain private counsel, and court-appointed attorneys had not yet been assigned. Prosecutors or police officers participated even less often than defense attorneys except in homicide cases when investigating detectives might come to arraignments to review the evidence with judges.

Arraignments and the accompanying bail hearings normally were undertaken by judges on a rotating basis in addition to other work assignments. During 1972, however, the presiding judge decided he would conduct arraignments during the week when sessions were held twice daily; as a consequence over 50 percent of the sampled pretrial release decisions were made by him. Other Recorder's Court judges and the visiting judges handled weekend and holiday arraignments or substituted for the presiding judge when he was unable to hold arraignments because of other court duties. The remaining 12 judges, then, accounted for 39 percent of the bails and the rest were set by visiting judges.

Arraignments and bail hearings took only about two minutes from start to finish, oftentimes even less than this. Cases were moved swiftly because the judges had other duties to perform and because the dockets generally were long. The presiding judge, for example, accepted 955 guilty pleas in 1972 (13 percent of all pleas for the year) and held six jury trials in addition to the rest of his responsibilities.[23] With arraignments and bail hearings making up only part of their workloads judges spent as little time as possible on them. They were encouraged to do so, moreover, by the fact that slightly more than 11,800 felony defendants were arraigned in 1972 so that the average bail docket numbered approximately 19 defendants for each session, or about 38 cases a day.

The court's limited detention resources also may have encouraged speedy completion of the hearings. There was little reason to spend a great deal of time processing numerous minor felony cases, such as carrying a concealed weapon, because to avoid overcrowding in the jail these defendants virtually were assured of personal bonds or recognizance. (Of the sample defendants with weapon offenses 75 percent were granted recognizance.) At the other extreme, when the charge was first degree murder, the bail hearing also became extremely truncated since defendants generally were automatically remanded. (Seventy-four percent of the sample defendants were denied bail.) The absence of attorneys, finally, facilitated brief hearings and hence their routinization. When they took part in the proceedings, they invariably took longer to complete.

Although arresting officers were rarely in the courtroom for arraignments, a nonuniformed officer on permanent assignment to the court was responsible for gathering information about defendants for the judges. The Release on Recognizance Program was not directly involved in bail decisions. Defendants were not interviewed prior to being arraigned nor did investigators make bail recommendations. At bail hearings their task, which was done in a room adjacent to the courtroom, was to register defendants granted personal bonds so that they could be notified about their court dates.

Quick routine decision making, in summary, was characteristically the way pretrial release options were chosen in Recorder's Court. Dockets were large and comprised of felonies, many of which could be processed almost automatically in part because space in the jail was limited. Judges were able to hurry through the proceedings because they normally did not have to interact with defense counsel or prosecutors, and their other responsibilities on the bench put a premium on the amount of time they could afford to spend on them. A final factor is that they did not have to search for information. The arraignment officer did this for them and equally as important condensed the information and highlighted its more salient aspects. The brevity of the hearings thus gains particular importance because even though information in Detroit was plentiful and reliable the judges did not thoroughly review it. Instead, they tended to rely on summaries prepared by the arraignment officer.

Information and the Role of the Arraignment Officer

Recorder's Court's location in the Frank Murphy Hall of Justice along with the prosecutor's office, court clerk, and probation department, all organizations producing and storing information relevant to bail decisions, eased the problem of collecting this information. Besides its accessibility, this information was relatively complete and current. The prosecutor had material on the criminal incident, the prior record of defendants, and the Warrant Section's assessments of cases. The clerk's office kept the records on case histories which were used to determine whether defendants had pending cases before the court as well as dispositions of any earlier cases. If defendants were on probation, the probation department had its own set of files and information.

The arraignment officer was responsible for collecting this information for the judges. Before bail hearings he went to the Warrant Section for the files on defendants to be arraigned. If relevant disposition information was missing, he checked with the clerk's office or probation department. After pulling together this information and reviewing it for discrepancies or errors, he filled out forms summarizing and spotlighting its major features and attached them to the front of the files. During bail hearings he stood beside the bench and as each defendant came forward handed the file to the judge. In most instances, the judge had seen neither the file nor the officer before the start of the proceedings and so, as the defendant walked to the bench, he or she would glance hurriedly at the summary form. This expedited the flow of work, but it also enhanced the officer's role in the bail decision because the attention judges gave the files was focused or directed by him.

The summary forms, for example, indicated whether defendants were wanted on other arrest warrants or if they had been "cooperative" with the police written in "large red letters" according to one judge. The officer also alerted judges when defendants had pending criminal cases and what the bails were in these cases, whether they used aliases, if they had outstanding warrants for failing to appear in court, and if they were on parole or probation. Directing the judges' attention to these matters affected bail decisions. For example, the association (gamma) between receiving personal bonds or cash bails and whether defendants were on bond for another offense was $-.54$; it was $-.50$ when they had a case pending in court; −.37 if they used an alias; and −.21 if they were on probation or parole. Therefore, by regularly advising judges about these factors, the arraignment officer could play a significant part in affecting the punitiveness of bail decisions.

The arraignment officer also may have conveyed bail requests by the police to the judges. How frequently or under what conditions this happened could not be determined and only one instance of such requests was observed. A $5,000 surety bond was imposed on a woman charged with carrying a concealed weapon. For most defendants with this charge, bail usually was personal bond. In chambers afterward the judge said the woman was a "beard" for a man whom the police were investigating for several crimes, including bank robbery, and that the police "attitude" had been important in his decision. A "beard," he explained, was a person with no prior record who agreed to carry a gun for someone else with the understanding that if arrested he or she would be given bail money.

When interviewed the judges did not view the officer's responsibilities as including bail recommendations. But at least one regularly sought his opinions. During one morning session, the judge asked on three separate occasions if the officer had any objection to personal bonds. During another session the judge inquired, "Any request for bond?" Since the charge was attempted rape of a minor, the officer replied, "I would suggest a big bond under the circumstances." In general, however, judges perceived the arraignment officer as simply a source of reliable information. For example, after learning he was retiring from the police department, a judge interrupted the proceedings and instructed the court reporter to take down "for the record" a short speech extolling the officer as "always a source of good information." Another said in an interview that he felt the officer did not consider himself an agent for the department or that his purpose was to represent its interests. He saw the arraignment officer as helping him rather than a source of police pressure.[24]

Honesty Tests and Situational Justice

After arraigning a defendant and having looked at the summary form, judges often simply told him what the bail would be and ended the hearing. The defendant, silent except when asked what his plea was to the charge, then was guided by the guards to the Release on Recognizance representative or taken to jail. On other occasions when judges asked defendants one or more questions before announcing their decisions, they were testing the defendant's honesty. Honesty tests were not an invariable feature of Detroit's process, although the presiding judge in 1972 regularly, if somewhat perfunctorily, incorporated them into his routine.

These tests generally involved questions about the defendant's criminal record. One reason for this was that copies of the records were in the files and this gave judges reasonably reliable data to check a defendant's response. Second, the defendant's response regarding prior arrests were less ambiguous than answers to other questions focusing on employment or marital status. A yes or no answer, a complete or incomplete response to questions about earlier brushes with the law immediately indicated when defendants were being honest. Replies to other kinds of questions might be more vague and less succinct, forcing judges to spend more time if they wanted to find out just what kind of employee the defendant was or how stable his marriage might be. Dishonest answers to questions about previous arrests or convictions, on the other hand, clearly signaled when defendants could not be trusted.

Two examples of honesty tests will be presented. The first one took place before the presiding judge. The second involved a black judge who granted personal bonds to nearly 70 percent of the 42 sample defendants he arraigned. The presiding judge after telling the defendant he was charged with stealing a car, accepting his not guilty plea, and determining whether he wanted an assigned attorney, then asked the defendant:

"Have you ever been arrested anywhere in the world since the day you were born to this day?" The defendant replied that he was arrested two or three years ago. "What for?" "I forget," the defendant answers.

"Weren't you arrested this year. In April? Weren't you in the Wayne County Jail for a day or so? On the 26th?" The judge asks the questions without giving the defendant a chance to reply.

After pausing for a moment, the judge informed the defendant he had a "pretty bad memory" and added, "Have to have a bondsman for people with bad memories." He set surety bail at $1,000.

The defendant then spoke up and told the judge that he hadn't thought it was very important to remember the charge in the earlier case. The judge smiles. "You didn't think it was very important? Well, bond isn't either."

Usually the judge did not badger defendants as he did here. An illustration of his more typical and abbreviated style of setting bails involved a case where the defendant was accused of larceny by trick involving $1,925. When the defendant replied he couldn't remember if he had ever been arrested "anywhere in the world from the day you were born to the present," he was told, "People with poor memories have high bonds," and bail was set at $10,000. From start to finish the encounter took less than half a minute.

In the next example, the defendant trying to put a box of bicycles evidently stolen from a nearby boxcar into his car was caught by a Penn Central Railroad security guard. After arraigning him and finding out if he could hire his own attorney, the following exchange took place between the defendant and the judge.

The judge asks the defendant if he has been in any trouble before. The defendant says that he had an armed robbery before his honor back in 1969. "Are you on probation or parole at present?" "No sir, not right now."

"Married?" "No, but I have a daughter I take care of." "Do you work?" The defendant says he does at a Clark gas station and gives the address.

The judge returns to the defendant's record. "Have you been in any trouble since '69?" The defendant says no. The judge then ask if the defendant was sentenced for armed robbery in '72. The defendant admits this is so, but it was a probation violation for the charge in '69.

With anger in his voice, the judge tells the defendant, "Why did you say that you weren't in any trouble since '69? And what about this? Weren't you convicted of breaking into a boxcar in '72? If you hadn't lied, I would have had a little mercy. But I can't stand people lying to me!"

Bond was set at $2,000.

Judges deliberately employed these tests. During an interview, while discussing the various considerations that went into his bail decisions, a judge without prompting included the defendant's honesty. He said he used different "ploys" to elicit the truth from defendants and that it was a "psychological game." Honesty tests were constructed opportunities for self-impeachment by defendants. If they failed them, they confirmed the appropriateness of their criminal stigma plus defying the authority of the court. Questions as to whether they could be trusted not to commit additional crimes if released or whether they would appear in court were answered by their own lack of candor.

Defense Attorneys and the Bargaining Mode

Bargaining over pretrial release decisions need not involve a series of requests by an attorney and counterproposals by a prosecutor or judge before they finally settle on a decision. It also may take place when defense attorneys, by offering different interpretations of the facts in cases or submitting additional information, challenge the evidence and inferences drawn by judges regarding the culpability of defendants. In other instances, however, bargaining can be more implicit and quite simply be a favor to the attorney granted by the judge.

Detroit's judges felt defense attorneys could be very helpful if they were at arraignments. They presumed attorneys discussed the cases with their clients beforehand and thus could offer contrasting opinions about the strength of evidence or different views of alleged incidents. One attorney questioned this presumption and thought that just by being at the arraignment with his client judges would see that the defendant had made an "investment" in his case and that this was more important in the outcome of the hearing than anything he might say. He argued there was too little time before arraignments to learn much about cases. The arraignment officer did not arrive in the courtroom until shortly before the bail hearings began and consequently he rarely saw the files or what the police had in the case. Without some knowledge about this information, talking to his client was not especially useful since he might not be honest or know what evidence the prosecutors had. His experience, he concluded, proved that "just being there" as a symbol of his client's concern was enough to get a lower bail.

His argument and conclusion appear to be borne out in the following cases. An attorney whose client had been arraigned on breaking and entering an occupied dwelling told the judge he considered the cash bail of $5,000 to be "pretty big" for this kind of charge. The judge disagreed and explained to him that a month ago he had put the defendant on probation for another offense and now he was back in court plus being in violation of his probation. Apparently unaware of his client's situation, the attorney replied, "Oh, I didn't know." Defense attorneys obviously could be handicapped by the limited information at their disposal during arraignments in arguing for less punitive bails.

In other instances, as the following two examples illustrate, bargaining involved granting favors to attorneys.

The defendant was charged with stealing an automobile. Defense counsel tells the judge he and his father have known the defendant and his family for many years and that he and his father will take personal responsibility for the appearance of the defendant.

The attorney tells the judge the defendant has been in the city "all his life." The judge notes the defendant has an address in Akron. The attorney then explains the defendant had worked there, but was back in the city. The judge takes the discrepancy lightly.

"Well, you know our policy. You get one every six years. Both you and your father are betting on this one. But just remember if he doesn't show, you don't get another one for six years. We give them out only once every six years."

The defendant was granted personal bond.

In the next case before a different judge the defendant was accused of robbery with a deadly weapon and felonious assault.

The attorney tells the judge he knows the defendant, "how his mind works," and asked for a low bail.

The judge responds that the victim was shot and this is a "bad" case in that the witness who was in court when the warrant was signed saw the defendant shoot the victim twice.

The judge reads the report. Looking up from his file, he tells the attor-

ney that the defendant stood over the victim and shot him after the victim had fallen.

"Has to be a surety, but I'll make it as low as possible," the judge concludes. Bond was set at $1,500.

In the first example the judge, running for reelection, alluded to this when he mentioned how frequently he granted personal bonds under these circumstances. The second illustration involved more serious charges. The attorney's presence appears to have been extremely important in reducing what normally would have been a much more costly bail decision since the median bail for just armed robbery was $5,000 for the sample defendants.

A Brief Recapitulation

Bail decisions in Detroit were made through all three modes of choice—routine, situational, and bargaining—with the routine mode predominating. Heavy judicial workloads, lengthy arraignment dockets, numerous relatively minor felony cases where recognizance release was almost automatic, the normal absence of attorneys and prosecutors, and reliable information summarized by the arraignment officer either encouraged or facilitated routinization of bail hearings in Recorder's Court. Earlier studies of bail are replete with complaints that bail procedures and decisions tend to be mechanical and routinized as if to suggest that the stringency or liberality of pretrial release policies reflected solely the nature of the decision process.[25] A major flaw in the implied argument that reforming decision processes will change policies is that it fails to take into account external influences on the court's bail tariff, and that it is possible that a court's tariff may change *without* altering the character of its bail-setting process. In other words, the contextual factors encouraging the use of particular decision modes in many instances are separable from those shaping bail tariffs. In Detroit the jail suit exerted a critical impact on Recorder's Court's tariff. It is time now to investigate how the court reacted to this challenge.

ENVIRONMENTAL CHALLENGES AND THE PROCESS OF POLICY CHANGE

Dramatic growth on Recorder's Court's dockets in the late 1960s and early 1970s set the stage for its reaction to the reduction in detention resources and shaped its policy changes during this time. Caseloads had begun to mount two years before the riot, as shown in Figure 3.1 which indicates the annual number of felony warrants issued and arraignments conducted in Detroit from 1960 through 1973.[26]

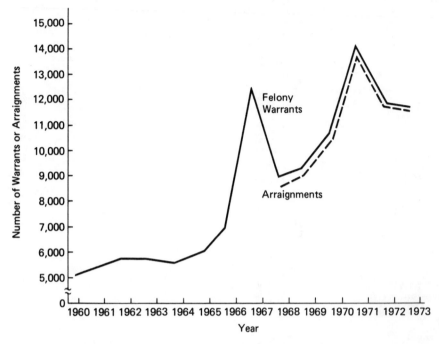

FIGURE 3.1   Number of Felony Warrants and Defendants Arraigned on Felony Charges in Detroit, 1960–1973.

The effects of restoring order to the riot torn city gave this trend an abrupt upward twist in 1967. The prosecutor's office ceased its normal review of felony warrants during the riot thus removing the sieve that screened warrant requests and producing a torrent of felony defendants. As one prosecutor put it.

> In July [during the riot] we didn't reject any warrants. When you have 4,800 warrants coming in in a period of a week, you obviously don't have time to interview witnesses, or the defendant . . . so you sign the warrant. In the normal course of events we don't consider ourselves a rubber stamp for the police, [but] in July it's no secret that we rejected very few warrants.[27]

Although the 1968 caseload dropped considerably from this peak, it failed to return to preriot levels. In fact it resumed its climb until the annual total reached an unprecedented high of nearly 14,300 warrants in 1971. For the next two years the number of warrants fell below this record volume, but still exceeded any other previous year's totals. Arraignments, of course, followed the path blazed by the warrant trends.

The steep rise in caseload in 1967 is readily explainable by the law enforcement reaction to the riot, but what of 1971 when the number of arraignments leaped by 3,000 over the previous year? Table 3.1 indicating the composition of the court's dockets for 1970–1973 suggests that other

TABLE 3.1 Composition of Bail Dockets in Detroit, 1970–1973

Charge at Arraignment	1970		1971		1972		1973	
	Number of Defendants	Percent	Number of Defendants	Percent	Number of Defendants	Percent	Number of Defendants	Percent
Weapons	1,184	11.2	2,050	14.7	2,255	19.0	2,277	19.7
Narcotics	1,274	12.0	3,042	21.9	2,333	19.7	2,256	19.5
Property	4,811	45.5	5,252	37.7	3,634	30.7	3,261	28.2
Personal	2,654	25.1	2,753	19.8	2,616	22.1	2,671	23.1
Other	651	6.1	818	5.9	1,000	8.5	1,099	9.5
Totals	10,574	99.9	13,905	100.0	11,838	100.0	11,564	100.0

SOURCE: Recorder's Court of the City of Detroit, *Annual Reports*.

factors lay behind this second dramatic increase in docket size, factors, however, that also reflected law enforcement policies.

Between 1970 and 1971 the combined proportions of persons arraigned on property and personal crime, although increasing slightly in absolute terms, dropped from about 71 to 57 percent of all persons arraigned in court. Meanwhile, the proportion accounted for by defendants with narcotics charges rose by nearly 10 percentage points and for those arraigned on weapon warrants by 3.5 points. Numerically, the size of these two groups of defendants more than doubled. Most of the growth in the docket, then, reflected sharp rises in the number of defendants accused of either narcotics offenses (mostly possession charges) or carrying a concealed weapon. Compared to other kinds of offenses, these charges reflect a more vigorous use of police discretion in apprehending offenders and are usually "proactive" decisions rather than simply "reactive" responses to citizen complaints. As Wilson has argued, proactive decisions are amenable to departmental priorities, and sudden changes in such arrests often spring from policy decisions made at higher levels.[28] It is justifiable to assume then that some time during 1970–1971, perhaps earlier, the Detroit Police Department, probably in conjunction with the prosecutor's office, decided to press for greater enforcement of narcotic and weapon laws. The result quite clearly shows up in the sudden jump in the number of persons arraigned on these charges in 1971.

When caseloads and defendant volumes grow as dramatically as they did in Detroit, pressures mount, sending shockwaves reverberating throughout the system. In particular, the jail would be expected to experience if not an equal than certainly a corresponding expansion in its jail population. As the number of felony defendants arraigned before Detroit's criminal bench mounted throughout this period, did the inmate population in the Wayne County Jail also grow?

Emergence of a Policy Puzzle: Trends in the Jail and Pretrial Release Rates

Overcrowding was an acute problem in Detroit's jail. As the tidal wave of defendants swept through Recorder's Court, it would be expected that it had grown worse. In fact, it did not. As indicated by Figure 3.2, which plots the average daily population of the jail from 1969–1973 (the 1968 average, regrettably, was unavailable), conditions in the jail at least in terms of population improved.

The jail's daily population remained very nearly the same for 1969 and 1970, about 1,400 prisoners, even though the number of arraignments had risen by almost 1,500 cases. And in 1971, when the number of arraigned felony defendants leapt to new heights, the jail population dropped! Moreover, this decline continued until 1973 when the average daily population was only about half that of 1971 and a scant 40 percent

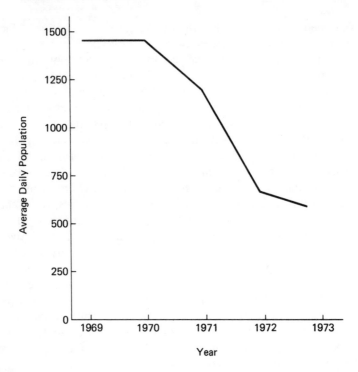

FIGURE 3.2 Average Daily Population of the Wayne County Jail, 1969–1973.

of the 1969–1970 average. Before 1972 the jail had been overcrowded; but with its legal limit set at 813 inmates, it could be viewed as actually underutilized afterward. The drop in 1972, of course, followed the judgment in the jail case that after December 31, 1972 the jail population could not exceed its rated capacity or the sheriff would be held in contempt of court. With Recorder's Court cases accounting for nearly two-thirds of the jail's population the judges had to take steps to do something about this problem; by 1972 this meant increasing the use of recognizance release or personal bonds.

This seemingly obvious step, however, followed a not so obvious sequence of policy adjustments by the court as it juggled its set of conflicting demands and pressures. In Chapter 2 it was argued that bail policy change in many instances may be the last, not the first, resort of courts, and such was the case in Detroit. Thus, the puzzle is not so much why Recorder's Court began to grant recognizance more liberally to felony defendants, but how it was able to cope with a mounting burden of work and problems in the jail *without* changing its bail practices until the last minute. In sorting out the pieces to this puzzle, it is best to begin with a look at the pretrial policies employed by Recorder's Court during this time and at the operation of its surety bond market.

Over a period of four years, the proportion of felony defendants granted recognizance release by Recorder's Court stayed very stable even as bail dockets quickly expanded, the mix of offenses changed, and the jail remained overcrowded. From 1968 to 1971 the recognizance rate steadily averaged 33 to 34 percent; only after the population lid was clamped on the jail did it shoot up to 48 percent. Figure 3.3 makes an interesting point, however, because it suggests that the court's tardiness in making this change actually may have made it more, not less, difficult to grapple with its jail problem because the overall release rate for defendants was falling during this period. In 1968, 85 percent of the arraigned defendants were freed pending disposition of their cases; but by 1971 the percentage had dropped to 71 percent.

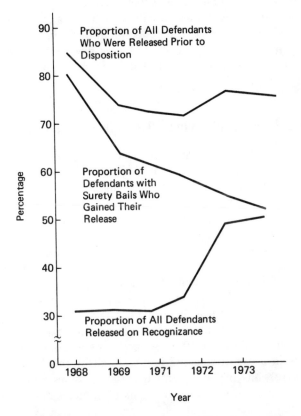

FIGURE 3.3   Release Rates for Felony Defendants in Detroit, 1968–1973.

The critical factor behind this decline was the collapse of Detroit's surety market. In 1968 about 81 percent of all defendants who needed to post surety bonds were able to use the intercessions of bondsmen to gain their release. From this high-water mark the rate dropped continuously until it sank to only about 50 percent in 1973. In 1971, when the volume of defendants hit its peak, the surety release rate had fallen to about 58 percent. The magnitude of this change should not be passed over quickly. In six years the release rate for defendants with surety bails plummeted by 30 percentage points! The reasons for this steady deterioration in the performance or efficiency of Detroit's bonding market are a bit obscure. Later in Chapter 4 when the surety markets in Detroit and Baltimore are compared, an explanation for Detroit's poorer performance in 1972 will be offered, but the analysis does not include earlier years.

Whatever the causes behind these trends, the fact remains that prior to 1972 the court's pretrial release policies and Detroit's surety markets did not help in solving, and indeed may have exacerbated, problems in the jail. If the court was not actively looking for or adopting bail policies that would reduce the influx of defendants into the jail, then the detention population trends during this period must have reflected court efforts aimed at accelerating the outflow of detained defendants. This next piece in the puzzle needs a closer look.

Minimizing the Risks of Change: The Role of Dispositional Slack

An earlier reference to visiting judges in Detroit provides a clue to what was happening during this time. These judges were first assigned to Recorder's Court by Michigan's Supreme Court in 1969. In fact, beginning that year Detroit's court adopted a number of policies that successfully maintained and then altered the balance between the inflow and outflow of prisoners affecting the jail's population. Prompted initially by the court's long backlog of untried cases (to some extent a carryover from the 1967 riot) and by conditions in the jail, they were instituted by the court in three stages. During the first phrase, encompassing 1969 and 1970, it attempted to quicken the pace at which it disposed of its cases.

Jail problems—overcrowding, physical deterioration, unsanitary conditions—were not new issues in Detroit. The need for a new jail had been voiced by a public official in 1967, by the National Council on Crime and Delinquency in a report released in 1968, and by the Michigan Department of Corrections in 1969. With these expressions of concern in the background and faced with its own backlog problems and delays in completing its trial docket, Recorder's Court announced in 1969 its participation in the visiting judge program which expanded its personnel resources to combat these problems.[29] As a further step, the bench also started to encourage more guilty pleas to hasten the movement of cases. The year before this announcement 55 percent of Detroit's felony defendants pleaded guilty. By 1970 the guilty plea rate had risen to 60 percent.[30] These two changes probably helped to move cases more swiftly with the result that the jail's average daily population in 1970 nearly equaled the 1969 average despite the 15 percent increase in the number of defendants who were arraigned in Recorder's Court.

The second stage began the following year in 1971 when Recorder's Court changed its disposition priorities and created a release on recognizance program. During this year recall that the jail population began to decline despite the sharp upswing in the court's caseload and the continuing stability of its bail policies. Some of this decline undoubtedly was due to the court's expanded resources, but perhaps the most important contribution was made when the court reversed its disposition priorities which occurred, it might be noted, after the jail suit was filed in January 1971. Detroit traditionally had placed a higher priority on trying defendants who were out on bail than on jailed defendants on the assumption that prosecuting freed defendants first reduced the chances that they would commit additional crimes. Confronted with a rapidly mounting caseload, even with additional personnel on the bench and more guilty pleas, this "freed first" rule prevented the court from trying enough of the jail's population quickly enough to keep pace with the daily influx of new prisoners.

Caught between its responsibility for the jail's overcrowding and community fears over crime, Recorder's Court hesitated to widen its use of recognizance in order to stem the flow of defendants into the jail. As it explained in the *Annual Report* for the year:

> Externally, the court's task during 1971 was complicated by the overcrowded conditions at the Wayne County Jail. The public, none-the-less, clamored for protection from recidivistic felons.[31]

The jail complaint led Recorder's Court to reconsider its disposition priorities, but further political pressure was created by a suicide in the jail, several other attempts, and a death from causes related to poor health facilities; plus, of course, the attention these events reaped from the newspapers. With few choices left open to it, except revising its bail tariff, the court switched its trial priorities to "jailed first" and stated in its *Annual Report*:

> New priorities in the assignment of cases for trial were developed. Precedence was given to jail cases to the *virtual exclusion* of cases where the defendant was at liberty pending trial [emphasis added].[32]

The nearly 20 percent drop in the average daily jail population between 1970 and 1971 reveals the effectiveness of this change. Also, the court's new Release on Recognizance (ROR) Program may have had some impact after it started in February 1971. No data, however, were available on how many defendants the program actually released through its own efforts for this year. But it is important to note the program's personnel did not participate in the bail hearings held at arraignment—a key point in the proceedings in reducing the flow of defendants into the jail. Instead, they interviewed defendants who failed to make bail which could affect the outflow of defendants.

Little slack remained in Detroit's disposition processes by the time judgment was rendered in the jail case. Guilty pleas accounted for 94 percent of its convictions, compared to 84 percent in 1968. Bench personnel had been bolstered by the visiting judges who handled 21 percent of the court's total dispositions in 1972. An ROR Program had been established and disposition priorities reversed. Some idea of how these changes improved the speed with which Recorder's Court moved its docket, and hence accelerated the outflow of prisoners in the jail, can be found in its 1968 *Annual Report* where the court said:

> In bail cases the average length of time involved from inception to completion is approximately six months. In jail cases the time is approximately three months.[33]

In striking contrast the median number of days from arrest to courtroom disposition for Eisenstein and Jacob's sample of defendants in 1972 was a mere 71 days—about two months and a week from start to finish.[34] For those defendants detained for the entire predisposition period the median was just 27 days. In a span of five years Recorder's Court had slashed from two to four months off its disposition times.

When Circuit Court decreed in March 1972 that the jail population had to be reduced, the only option left open to Detroit's criminal court was changing its recognizance practices. With only nine months before the ruling went into effect, the court had little time to make further changes in its disposition processes that would boost the jail's turnover rate to the point where its daily population, which averaged 1,127 in 1971, would not exceed the jail's capacity limit by the end of the year. Yet, despite both the ruling and its limited options, Recorder's Court still hesitated to revise its bail policies until the middle of 1972, as indicated by Figure 3.4.

According to the presiding judge in 1971, the jail case "brought home the conditions of the jail to the bench" and he added that the judges decided personal bonds would have to be granted more extensively since Recorder's Court was "responsible for the vast majority" of the jail's inhabitants. Figure 3.4 indicates an upward trend in the proportion of felony defendants released on recognizance began in 1971, but shows it was quite irregular and not until the last six months of 1972 did it level off at about 52 percent. This suggests that, despite the unanimity of concern expressed by Detroit's judges, many still harbored some reluctance to reduce their use of surety bonds and switch to recognizance. It also may be the case that the bench did not fully or immediately appreciate the implications of the jail ruling and it took awhile before a consensus emerged as to what the court should do.

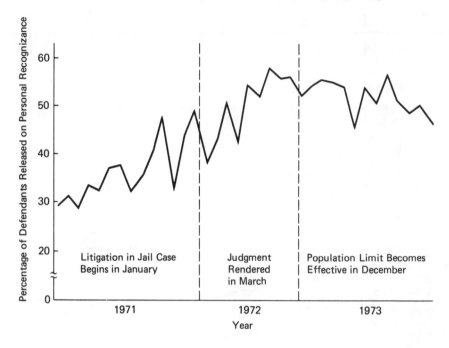

FIGURE 3.4   Monthly Trends in Percentage of Personal Recognizances Granted to Felony Defendants in Detroit.

Another factor discouraging the court's use of personal bonds was the historically high capias rate for these bonds compared to surety bonds. The proportion of defendants with personal bonds for whom arrest warrants or capiases were issued because of failure to appear in court ranged from three to four times greater than that for defendants released on surety bonds for the years 1968–1971 as shown by Figure 3.5.

The problem arose in the first place because Recorder's Court did not notify defendants about their court dates and relied simply on a "signed promise" by defendants at arraignment that they would appear in court. The ineffectiveness of this procedure is clear from Figure 3.5. In September 1971 the Release on Recognizance program established a "follow-up section" in order to "check on the whereabouts of defendants and to keep defendants informed of their court dates." According to Figure 3.5, the program closed the gap between personal and surety bond capias rates, but the judges' experiences of having trial or hearing dockets delayed because of absent or tardy defendants probably weakened the credibility personal bonds as an effective bail option.

Until the middle of 1972, then, Recorder's Court postponed revisions of its bail policies and focused instead on quickening the its disposition. This choice had several political advantages ' court probably found appealing. It reduced the backlog, c'

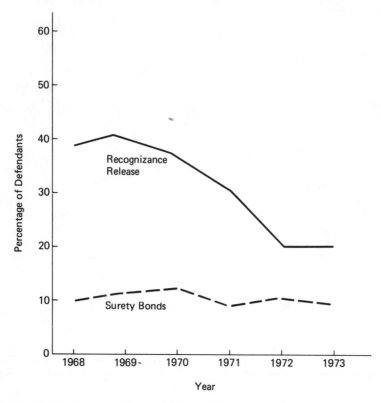

FIGURE 3.5   Reported Capias Rate by Type of Release, 1968–1973.

spent in jail for defendants who could not post bail, and lessened the probability of bail crime. Those demanding stern law enforcement were appeased because long predisposition periods often are thought to reduce the likelihood of convictions as victims and witnesses get discouraged, their memories fade, or change residences. Prodefendant groups were placated since defendants did not spend months in jail awaiting trial. Accordingly, shortening the time between arrest and trial became more enticing than liberalizing the use of recognizance. The jail case, however, not only compelled the court to take this step, but fortuitously came at a time when Recorder's Court held few options other than releasing substantially more defendants on their own recognizance.

CONCLUSIONS: TOWARD A POLITICAL CHOICE MODEL OF PRETRIAL POLICY CHANGE

By the end of 1972 half of Detroit's felony defendants were being freed n personal bond. Disposition procedures had been accelerated to the point where the median time from arraignment to disposition for jailed defendants was less than one month. These changes greatly reduced the breadth of the court's pretrial sanctions and lessened their severity. From the standpoint of elaborating the basic choice model outlined in Chapter 2, the string of events and conditions surrounding them also provide empirical material for a more complex model of policy change. Figure 3.6 depicts this model.

A court's pretrial policies emerge as political demands and expectations are weighed against detention capabilities. Mounting caseloads and other factors can upset this balance, but neither bail nor disposition policies need be changed so long as there is enough jail slack to soften the impact of these changes. In the event the jail becomes overcrowded (and this appraisal is fundamentally a political judgment reflecting the mood and character of the court's environment), the court may begin to re-evaluate its policies. At this point, it faces a number of choices each of which carries political consequences. The argument in Chapter 2 was that courts prefer to revise policies or practices that will satisfy their environment and minimize the risk of sanctions. Given the existence of disposition slack, measures cutting courtroom delay will be adopted rather than liberalizing bail policies. To some extent, however, this choice depends on whether the court also sets bail for large numbers of misdemeanants since they can be released more easily on recognizance than alleged felons, and the court may prefer to maintain its existing disposition procedures to avoid ruffling its relations with defense attorneys and prosecutors. If this opportunity exists, bail reform in the guise of pretrial release agencies may be adopted to help reduce the jail population. When the docket is filled with felony cases, however, the speedy trial option becomes an attractive alternative to bail changes.

The amount of slack in a court's disposition process, the effectiveness of the new program in reducing it, and the persistence of concern over the jail influence whether the court will have any further steps. If it finds additional changes are needed, it will continue to look in the neighborhood of those policy areas affecting the outflow of jailed defendants. Disposition priorities may be reversed and bail reviews instituted, as Detroit illustrated, before the court changes its release practices at arraignment. If these efforts fail, the court must consider liberalizing its bail policies by limiting the use of surety bonds or by lowering their customary amounts. Recognizance, however, is a more efficient solution to overcrowding than this option since some defendants inevitably will fail to make even the most meager money bail, and security or 10 percent deposit bails, although they remove the bondsman from the scene, may not produce dramatically different release rates compared to sureties.[35]

A court's decision to change its bail policy depends on the balance of concern expressed by important actors in the court's environment regarding continued overcrowding of the jail versus the fear of crime in the city.

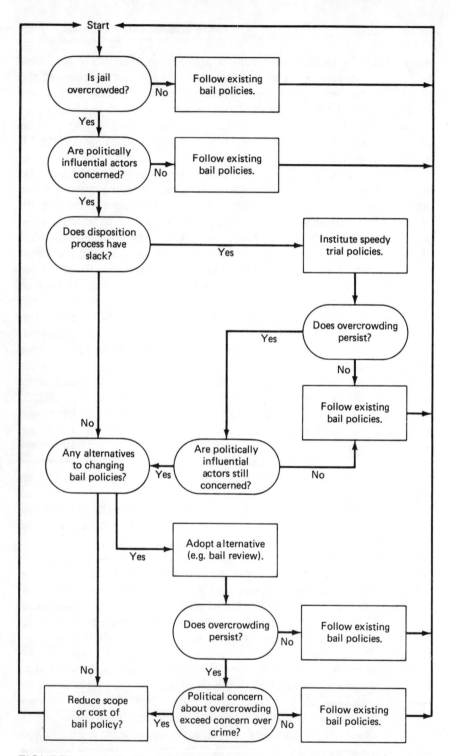

FIGURE 3.6 A Political Choice Model of Pretrial Punishment.

In the instance of Detroit, this balance was tipped decisively by the judgment in the jail case. Moreover, by the time this decision was made, the jail had developed a sufficiently notorious reputation that Recorder's Court probably perceived that jail conditions were a paramount issue in Detroit despite the gravity of its crime problem. If overcrowding, however, is seen as less important than the crime problem, the court will continue to follow its existing bail practices. This means that since overcrowding is tolerated the court is given the slack it needs to support these practices and that overcrowding will decline only as changes in the other variables affecting the inflow and outflow of jail prisoners change.

This model makes clear that bail policies are not static and that they do not follow automatically an evolutionary path toward reform in a rigid lockstep fashion. Environmental shocks may start a court moving along this path, but whether it completes this journey depends on the timing and sequence of events and the political conditions that exist at each of the major decision nodes. This point will become clearer in the next chapter which describes how overcrowding, jail rioting, and legal battles rocked the Baltimore City Jail, finally forcing the mayor to intercede, but produced few changes in the bail-setting process that existed in this city's lower court.

REFERENCES

1. Joel D. Aberbach and Jack L. Walker, *Race in the City*, Boston, Little, Brown and Company, 1973, pp. 54–55.
2. Edward C. Banfield, *Big City Politics*, New York, Random House, 1965, p. 51
3. Isaac D. Balbus, *The Dialectics of Legal Repression*, New York, Russell Sage Foundation, 1973, p. 114.
4. A highly critical account of this unit can be found in *Detroit under STRESS*, Detroit, From the Ground Up, 1973.
5. For an analysis of the role played by unions in Detroit politics, see J. David Greenstone, *Labor in American Politics*, New York, Vintage Books, 1969; and for the relationship between the unions and blacks, see James A. Geschwender, *Class, Race and Worker Insurgency*, Cambridge, Cambridge University Press, 1977; and August Meier and Elliott Rudwick, *Black Detroit and the Rise of the UAW*, New York, Oxford University Press, 1979.
6. Information on the court's response to the riot and judges' comments are taken from Balbus, *Dialectics*, pp. 119–121.
7. Donald I. Warren, *Justice in Recorder's Court: Report to the Equal Justice Council*, Detroit, Equal Justice Council, 1974.
8. A judge appointed to fill a vacancy on Recorder's Court who was campaigning for election for the remaining portion of the term mentioned during an interview that the alliance's screening panel asked him about his views on bail.
9. James Eisenstein and Herbert Jacob, *Felony Justice*, Boston, Little, Brown and Company, 1977, pp. 156–157.

10. *Wayne County Jail Inmates v. Wayne County Board of Commissioners*, Plaintiffs Complaint, p. 1.
11. Ibid., pp. 1–2.
12. Ibid., p. 2.
13. Subsequent litigation completed after 1972 reduced this population limit to about 700 inmates. It is also relevant to note that the Wayne County Jail housed prisoners from other courts in the county. As a result, the effective detention capacity available to Recorder's Court was actually less than the population limit. The court used as an informal guide the figure of about 550 prisoners to signal when it was reaching its maximum share of the jail's space. Another relevant aspect of the jail's capacity is that Recorder's Court reduced the number of convicted misdemeanants it sentenced to the Wayne County Jail in 1971 and 1972. In 1970 the Misdemeanor Division of the court sentenced 746 convicted misdemeanants to the jail. By 1971 this dropped to 298 and in 1972 it slipped to 190. One effect of the change was that it created space for Detroit felony defendants awaiting trial.
14. *Inmates v. Wayne County*, Plaintiffs Complaint, pp. 4–5.
15. *Detroit Free Press*, October 10, 1972.
16. Election data for this section are from the Detroit Election Commission, Official Canvass of Votes Cast at Primary and General Elections, 1968, 1972, and 1974.
17. Eisenstein and Jacob, *Felony Justice*, p. 141.
18. Ibid., pp. 144–145.
19. Erving Goffman's term is used here in the same way that Blumberg used it in *Criminal Justice*, Chicago, Quadrangle, 1967, pp. 110–115.
20. Data for the sample of defendants in Detroit indicated that 14 percent of the bail decisions made at arraignment were changed at subsequent stages in the disposition process; over 81 percent of these changes relaxed the stringency of the first decision; e.g., remands changed to cash bail, or bail amounts were reduced.
21. Lois Corman, "The Effect of Publicity on Bail Setting Behavior," unpublished paper, Pennsylvania State University, 1974.
22. See the appendix describing the field methods for the basis of this statement. Since most of the observations in Detroit were done in the summer of 1974, it may be wondered if bail setting in 1972 might not have been performed through other modes. Eisenstein and Jacob, and Luskin, however, found bail was usually a routinized procedure in 1972. See Eisenstein and Jacob, *Felony Justice*; and Mary Lee Muhlenkort Luskin, "Judging: The Effects of Experience on the Bench on Criminal Court Judges' Decisions," Ph.D. dissertation, Ann Arbor, University of Michigan, 1978.
23. Recorder's Court of the City of Detroit, Michigan, *Annual Report*, Detroit, Mich., 1972, p. 9.
24. The distinction between helping and pressure is drawn from Raymond A. Bauer, Ithiel de Sola, and Lewis Anthony Dexter, *American Business and Public Policy*, New York, Atherton Press, 1963.
25. See, for example, Legal Aid Society of New York City, "The Unconstitutional Administration of Bail: Bellamy v. the Judges of New York City," *Criminal Law Bulletin*, 8 (July–August 1972): 459–506.

26. Although arraignment volumes better measure the court's actual caseloads because some warrants do not result in arrest and subsequent arraignment (the proportion averaged 3.5 percent for 1968–1973), data on arraignments for the first part of the 1960s were not available.

27. Balbus, *Dialectics*, p. 117.

28. James Q. Wilson, *Varieties of Police Behavior*, Cambridge, Harvard University Press, 1968.

29. Recorder's Court cited a "grossly overcrowded" jail, a "record backlog," and "delays" as reasons for its participation in the program; see Recorder's Court of the City of Detroit, *Annual Report*, Detroit, Mich., 1969, p. 1.

30. Recorder's Court, *Annual Report*, Detroit, Mich., 1969, and 1970.

31. Recorder's Court, *Annual Report*, Detroit, Mich., 1971, p. 1.

32. Ibid.

33. Recorder's Court, *Annual Report*, Detroit, Mich., 1968, p. 1.

34. Eisenstein and Jacob, *Felony Justice*, p. 291.

35. Roy B. Flemming, C. W. Kohfeld, and Thomas M. Uhlman, "The Limits of Bail Reform: A Quasi-Experimental Analysis," *Law and Society Review*, 14 (Summer 1980): 947–976.

4

Choosing Between Risk and Reform: Felony Bail Processes in Baltimore

INTRODUCTION

After entering the offices of Baltimore's Pre-Trial Release Division, located on a busy downtown street across from the massive and ornate courthouse, a defendant in 1972 probably would have spotted a quotation tacked on the waiting room's wall. From Machiavelli it read: "There is nothing more difficult to take in hand, more perilous to conduct, or more uncertain to success than to take the lead in a new order of things."

Machiavelli's warning to reformers provides a clue to the situation that faced the new District Court commissioners when they began to implement the court's liberal bail rule in the fall of 1971. The balance of incentives and inducements impinging on bail decisions in Baltimore was tipped against a thorough-going liberalization of pretrial release opportunities for felony defendants. Nonetheless they bore the responsibility for carrying out Rule 777's mandate that all criminal defendants (except those accused of capital offenses) were eligible for recognizance release if they were considered likely to appear in court. Their predicament was defining the meaning of reform in an inauspicious political setting.

This chapter explores the context and processes that influenced how the commissioners coped with their problem. As the sections outlining the political environment and the conditions under which bail-setting decisions were made indicate, commissioners were constrained in ways that fostered a satisficing definition of reform based on minimizing the risks and uncertainty of change. Within these constraints they then had to look for tangible cues or guidelines that would assist them in settling such nettlesome problems as what constitutes a reasonable cash bail. The result, it will be suggested, was a revision in the city's previous bail tariff, a change that in general benefited most felony defendants. Still these changes were relative to the historical and political context that prevailed in Baltimore; its bail-setting policies, it should be borne in mind, were more stringent and costlier than those in Detroit during 1972.

It is also pertinent to mention here that in contrast to Detroit where events involving the jail greatly determined the scope of pretrial punishment, Baltimore's jail crisis, which was severe, played little or no role in shaping the commissioners' behavior. This difference spotlights a critical distinction between the two cities. Jail conditions and bail policies were closely linked in Detroit; contractions in the scope of pretrial punishment came as a series of policy responses to overcrowding in the jail and ultimately the decision in the jail case. In Baltimore this link was less strong. The jail crisis did prompt the city's higher court, the Supreme Bench, to take steps intended to alleviate the jail's problems. But no steps were directed toward altering the initial bail decisions made in District Court. What was missing in Baltimore that would have forged closer ties between these decisions and the jail's problems was a legally imposed population limit on the jail. In large measure a crucial reason for this was the weakness of prodefendant sentiment in Baltimore and, hence, the corresponding strength of concern over crime spearheaded by the police and public officials that influenced both the commissioners' behavior and the way in which the jail crisis was finally resolved.

THE POLITICAL ENVIRONMENT OF BAIL SETTING IN BALTIMORE

Baltimore did not have the strong tradition of labor activism, black militancy, or political reform that shaped events involving criminal justice matters in Detroit. Its black community, for example, accounted for 46 percent of Baltimore's population in 1970, but a history of weak political participation, Republicanism within its middle class, and factional feuding, along with gerrymandering in the past to assure white dominance, had retarded the growth of its political power. According to Bachrach and Baratz, "[A]s late as 1965 the political system in Baltimore was, for all practical purposes, closed to the people in the 'dark ghetto'...."[1] Although conditions began to change somewhat during the late sixties, efforts to create militant black organizations faltered. The durable coalitions needed for success could not be formed, and the attempt "to transform covert grievances of the black population into issues was also abortive."[2] Finally, despite the arrest and mass detention through high bails of nearly 5,500 persons (most of whom were black) during the riot after Martin Luther King's assassination in April 1968, there was not the same kind of critical reaction and formation of groups that followed Detroit's 1967 riot.[3]

Baltimore's city council was elected on a partisan basis with three members from each of the city's six wards or districts. Solidly Democratic since 1927, there were occasional flashes that the once powerful ward machines that had dominated city politics and loomed large at the state level still existed although their strength was ebbing.[4] By 1972 blacks held 5 of the council's 18 seats. Whether it was the existence of these machines, the prior history of feeble political clout, or perhaps multiple-member rather than single-member districts, this representation did not match the proportion of blacks in Baltimore's voting age population. About 44 percent of this population was black in 1970, but the proportion of black city council members was only 28 percent. By comparison these proportions were nearly the same in Cleveland and St. Louis which also had large black populations and elected their city councils on a partisan ward basis.[5]

Baltimore's black community had made even more limited gains in the city's criminal justice system. Out of 22 judges in District Court only 2 were black (although 1 had been named administrative judge) and on the Supreme Bench 3 of the 20 judges were black. There were no black full-time public defenders, few black private defense attorneys, and only 5 of the State's Attorney's 88 professional positions were held by blacks. The state attorney, it is well to note, was black, but after barely gaining office in 1970 he lost his reelection bid when the Democratic Party refused to renominate him. Within such organizations as the Court Clerk's Office or Sheriff's Department where blacks in Detroit held high positions, whites predominated in Baltimore.[6] Only in the instance of the District Court commissioners, nearly half of whom were black, was there a rough approximation of the city's racial composition because of the court's chief judge's conscious efforts.

The black community was not totally impotent in Baltimore, but its hold on the reins of power was more tenuous than in Detroit. It is illuminating that no black leaders came to the defense of Rule 777 or the commissioners when the police began their barrage of criticism. Only when the city comptroller called for the removal of one of the black District Court judges for approving a commissioner's bail decision which led to the release of a defendant who later shot and killed a police officer did the Monumental City Bar Association, a black law group, publicly defend the court. Furthermore, there were no biracial groups in Baltimore comparable to Detroit's Urban Alliance or Team for Justice that attempted to use political strategies to change the operation or policies of the city's criminal justice system. Indeed even politically liberal groups were unexpectedly mute during the troubled period following the police officer's death. The chief judge noted during an interview that he heard nothing from the "ACLU or other liberal groups" that he thought would have spoken up for the "defense of criminals."

To a degree the lawsuit filed by the Legal Aid Bureau against the Baltimore City Jail in May 1971 stands out as an exception to what has been said so far.[7] Yet it is critical to note that this organization normally did not handle criminal law matters. It was only after its staff heard numerous complaints about the jail's conditions and treatment of prisoners, particularly after a prisoner riot in February 1971, that three of its attorneys decided to seek legal redress. The city's legal community or defense bar were not involved in this case in contrast to Detroit where, besides such organizations as the National Lawyers Guild, 32 individual attorneys and 13 firms including those with politically prominent members were listed as plaintiffs' attorneys in the original complaint. This lack of involvement in Baltimore reflected the relative absence of radical and politically active liberal lawyers in this city. It also paralleled the conservative approach of the city's defense bar, especially the Public Defender's Office which unlike its Detroit counterpart did not assume an adversary, prodefendant stance vis-à-vis the city's criminal justice system.[8]

The political base supporting the rights of defendants in Baltimore, then, was weaker in general than in Detroit. As a result, criminal justice issues were framed by Baltimore's media and elected officials in terms of fighting crime. The city comptroller, for example, proclaiming the need for more rigorous law enforcement, created a crime commission to air his views which already had received wide publicity. He urged the creation of a civilian police auxiliary similar to one during World War II because in his eyes the crime situation had reached "critical" proportions requiring an "all-out war."[9] On another occasion after a jail disturbance he called for the construction of "prisoner of war camps" in outlying counties. His proposal struck a sympathetic cord for a former president of the Jail Board, a body appointed by the mayor to set policy for the jail. He agreed with the comptroller's proposal because other forms of detention, such as community corrections, were inadequate since "there's no deterrent there, no punishment."[10]

Given this generally conservative political climate in Baltimore, the genesis of Rule 777 takes on particular importance in appreciating the role of the commissioners, the problems they faced, and the reactions of the police and others to liberalization of bail in the city. Rule 777 marked an unexpected, abrupt change in the ways bail had been determined in Baltimore's lower court. It was not a response to widespread dissatisfaction with traditional bail practices or bondsmen, nor did it evolve as a solution to overcrowding or other problems in the jail. Instead it was part of a larger conversion of Baltimore's lower court into the state's District Court system after the influential Baltimore *Sun* exposed an extensive traffic ticket-fixing operation in the former Municipal Court two years earlier.

While the rules for the new court were being drafted, a staff attorney for the rules committee decided to revise those pertaining to bail. Drawing upon the Federal Bail Reform Act of 1966, bail standards promulgated by the American Bar Association, and a study of Municipal Court bail practices by two local law professors, he incorporated the presumption of recognizance release and other reform elements into the initial draft of the bail rule. In an interview the attorney (who did not practice criminal law) said there had been no public demand that he was aware of for further reform much beyond that represented by Baltimore's pretrial release agency, but the opportunity was there and he decided to take advantage of it. The committee, he stated, gave Rule 777 only a cursory review; it "more or less breezed through" with few substantive changes. One provision that was struck early in the drafting process, which has special significance in light of subsequent events, pertained to the defendant's dangerousness or possible threat to the safety of the community as a consideration in bail deliberations. Only the likelihood of appearing in court remained as the criterion governing pretrial release conditions. As a result, Rule 777 became "one of the most liberal" bail rules in the country according to a faculty member at the University of Maryland Law School.

Reform, Reaction, and the Police

From the start the police, in particular the Fraternal Order of Police, were critical of the commissioners and Rule 777. In one respect this reflected their shrinking role in Baltimore's lower court and their changing relationship with its officials. On the other hand, the intensity of their criticism was fueled by the deaths of two officers killed by defendants freed on bail. While the police took the lead in attacking the lower court's new bail practices, they were joined by others. At various times over the two years following the inauguration of District Court, prosecutors, the city comptroller, a Supreme Bench judge, state legislators, and the newspapers either complained or expressed doubt about Rule 777. Because the police played such a highly visible and active role in leading this critical chorus, it is useful to trace briefly the evolution of the relationship between the police and the city's lower courts.

Until 1960 Baltimore's lower court had been a "police court" run by "highly political police magistrates" lacking formal legal training and selected by the city's state senators.[11] As early as 1923 an investigatory commission described the court as "undignified, corrupt, and unjust." Overt police dominance ended in 1960 when Municipal Court was created. The new judges, who had to be lawyers with at least five years of experience, were appointed by the governor but subsequently ran in citywide elections as their initial terms expired.[12] In a study of the court in 1964, informed observers claimed the court was unduly sensitive to political demands. Judges, they asserted, found it "impossible" to ignore the "possible political effect of an unpopular decision" in cases involving serious changes and were "frequently pressured to help politically powerful persons."[13]

Relations between Municipal Court and the police remained close during the 1960s. Following the police court tradition, judges continued to work in courtrooms located in the district police stations, making them easily accessible to officers. Nearness to the police went beyond more propinquity, however. Officers viewed the judges as partners in a "team" and as fellow "conservators of the peace," a view apparently accepted by most of the judges.[14] The police also performed important functions in the court such as serving as prosecutors in cases. In addition, they set bails using a bail schedule approved by the court. Throughout the brief life of Municipal Court there evidently was both "considerable pressure" on the judges to go along with police wishes, and a judicial willingness to do so.

The advent of District Court ruptured these traditionally close ties and eliminated the police role in bail decisions. The new chief judge, intent upon improving the image of Baltimore's lower court, told commissioners that they were not to think of themselves as partners with the police. The comment by a commissioner that he was a "buffer" between defendants and police reflected this injunction. For this same reason, the chief judge and administrative judge also refused to appoint any of the active or retired desk sergeants who, according to the judges, applied for the commissioner posts believing that their experience qualified them for the job. Thus, if the police wanted to detain or release a defendant, they would have to gain the cooperation of the commissioners. But, as the following comment by the administrative judge suggests, this change was not easy for the police.

> It is a tremendous change for the police. Before the District Court system came into being, a person was arrested and the bail was set by police off some list. If the person was unruly, the police could simply increase the charges—and the bail. Now the commissioner will look at the situation realistically and will release suspects on their own recognizance if he feels it is warranted.[15]

Signals by District Court that the commissioners would work independently of the police, loss of authority over bail decisions, and a liberal pretrial release rule created the backdrop for the next stage in the relationship between the police and the lower court. It was not long before the police tested this new relationship. And, when the shootings of the police officers occurred, they mounted a full-scale attack on the reform.

Three days after the commissioners started setting bails, police officers cited examples to newspaper reporters of defendants released on their own recognizance who formerly would have been detained, complaining this "leniency" encouraged them to commit new crimes without fear of the consequences.[16] Three months later, a district prosecutor, alarmed over bails that were "too low," accused the commissioners of "letting many, many shoplifters and possession of deadly weapon cases out on low bail or recognizance and these people just don't show up."[17] The police attack escalated in July of 1972 when the first patrolman was killed. The commissioner involved in the case had no difficulty recalling the incident, or the comment the city comptroller made on television that the commissioners were a "threat to the city." The volume of criticism subsided substantially, however, after an officer admitted he had asked for the bail so the defendant could continue to serve as a narcotics informant.[18]

In September following this incident, a Supreme Bench judge assailed the 10 percent security bond provision in Rule 777. When a man accused of breaking and entering failed to appear for trial after his girl-friend posted $150 of his $1,500 bond, the judge sharply criticized the procedure. "What the defendant has lost in putting up the $150 is probably less than the cost of retaining an attorney," the judge claimed. He concluded that this was a "pretty cheap way to avoid criminal prosecution."[19] Two days later the Baltimore *News-American* published a series of four articles on District Court's bail policies.

Prominently featured in the articles were the charges and accusations voiced by the police. The Fraternal Order of Police denounced the court as "permissive" and accused commissioners of "releasing back into the community criminals who have terrorized and harassed the people."[20] The State's Attorney Office concurred. Asserting its experience indicated "too many" defendants were committing more crimes while out on bail, it urged legislative changes in Rule 777 to allow preventive detention.[21] The commissioners were a "joke" the police said because they lacked the facilities and time required for a thorough investigation of defendants, and significantly it was felt that they did not ask the police often enough for information. An officer active in the FOP was quoted as saying:

> Often they don't have time to go into a suspect's prior record to determine if he's on probation. They don't check into his background, what type of neighborhood he's from. They don't speak with the police to find out about the people he is associating with.[22]

The president of the FOP singled out the absence of legal training among most of the commissioners; except for two, none of the remaining 25 commissioners was a lawyer. Consequently he charged they had "no concept of the severity of a crime," and asked, "How can they sit in judgment when they don't know the law?"[23]

The imminent demise of the former police-court team was portended by the administrative judge's response to these attacks. Because of them, he suggested the court might be less cooperative in releasing narcotic informers. According to the judge:

A lot of these defendants are repeaters. As a rule we don't release them unless release is recommended by the police department. Now the police won't find it so easy and accommodating. They [commissioners] are going to protect themselves from criticism.[24]

Despite this warning, the Fraternal Order of Police announced in April 1973 that it would resume its efforts to "either abolish the entire district court system or have it changed in order to protect the rights of the community as well as defendants."[25] This announcement came after a second policeman was slain by a defendant, who, according to the police, had been arrested 21 times in seven years and twice in the two months prior to this incident. The FOP also pointed out that one of these recent arrests involved an assault on a police officer. This incident revived public criticism by the police, but their relationship with the court had been deteriorating during the previous year. The FOP charged the chief judge had "completely ignored" its complaints about bail decisions made by commissioners and accused the administrative judge of being equally uncooperative because he refused to allow its members access to court records and files for a study it wanted to conduct of District Court.

In the meantime legislators from Baltimore started offering bills in Maryland's House of Delegates and its state Senate that would tighten the provisions of Rule 777. One bill required an automatic $50,000 bail for defendants charged with armed robbery. Another sought to revise Rule 777 so that a defendant's threat to the community could enter into formal consideration of bail.[26] Yet a third bill would have denied bail for certain crimes and was a response to Maryland's high court ruling that bail was permissible in capital offense cases.[27] None of these bills passed, but to delay the rush to change the state's bail rules, the chief judge of the District Court successfully bought time by urging a study of the effectiveness of Rule 777.[28] It was finally completed and published in 1974.[29]

Although the city's newspapers supported the need for the study, they expressed various misgivings about the impact of Rule 777 and urged that they be included in the study. The *News-American* hoped the study would answer questions that had been raised about the extent of bail crime.[30] The *Sun* after paying obeisance to the argument that bail was justified since defendants had not yet been tried, concluded: "While constitutional rights must be protected, many a person with a criminal record and out on bail pending a trial has been arrested and charged with additional crimes."[31]

Responsibility Without Power: The Vulnerability of Commissioners

The commissioners had few personal or institutional resources to buffer themselves from this threatening environment. Most were either former investigators for the Pre-Trial Release Division or former police officers.

Background information for 17 commissioners indicated that 7 had worked for the pretrial agency and 6 were with the police department before becoming commissioners. The remaining commissioners were drawn from occupations outside the criminal justice system. They earned $9,500 a year in 1972 and occupied the lowest rung of the District Court hierarchy. Appointed by the chief judge and serving at his pleasure, they lacked civil service protection and could be removed from office at any time.

Their major patron and protector was the chief judge. As one commissioner put it, "If it wasn't for him, we wouldn't be here." Still his support was not always enough, for, as the judge himself noted during an interview, the commissioners "tightened up" when the first patrolman was killed and the police intensified their assault on the court. Although he frequently appeared on television to rebut critics of Rule 777, his ability to defend the commissioners was somewhat limited because his offices were in Annapolis. The commissioners in any case perceived themselves as vulnerable to sanctions. One stated he thought the problem of defendants failing to appear when they were released was more common than defendants committing crimes before their trials, but the public and newspapers were more concerned with the latter. Without prompting he added that if this happened too often it would affect whether he kept his job. A second commissioner in describing his role as having "responsibility or authority, but no power," summed up the plight of the commissioners.

Baltimore's commissioners soon learned the rewards of caution and the limits of their autonomy. Working at the bottom of the court's hierarchy, for example, made them subject to reprimands from District Court judges. A commissioner who said he felt secure in his job nevertheless became uneasy when he heard through the court's grapevine that the judge sitting in the district during the day had gone over some of his decisions. After completing his review, the judge was reported to have wondered, "Perhaps _____ is afraid to set high bails." Another commissioner recalled that when a defendant failed to appear, a district judge questioned him closely about the decision and particularly whether he had checked the defendant's criminal record. He concluded from this experience that when "they start going over the papers and asking you questions, you better be able to remember what you were doing."

Media attention also taught them that their decisions might result in public exposure, criticism, or questions regarding their competence. A commissioner related a case when the police wanted a high bail for a reputedly prominent figure in organized crime so they could hold him for federal authorities. Because it was a minor charge, he refused to go along with the request and set bail at $1,000. The newspapers later published an account that, according to the commissioner, made him look "foolish." A second commissioner rather than denying bail for an accused murderer set a $50,000 cash bail. After leaving work, he found out the newspapers were printing articles about the case. He returned to the district, and to his relief, he said, the defendant had not made bail. He then changed the bail to a remand.

Finally, the commissioners, who besides their bail duties were responsible for handling warrants requested by citizens, discovered to their dismay that citizens unhappy with their decisions felt free to complain to district judges or the local media. For example, a commissioner talked about an incident when a woman started "raising a racket" after he refused to issue a warrant. He could tell she had been drinking. When he asked her about it, "she hit the roof and told me off." Shortly afterward she complained to the administrative judge about the commissioner's impudence. Another commissioner said he denied a warrant requested by a close relative of one of Baltimore's last ward bosses. She went to a local television station which aired her complaint. Even in bail cases commissioners found their authority questioned. A commissioner, following court custom, remanded a defendant charged with rape. The defendant's mother and her attorney were in court (an extremely rare occurrence in Baltimore). The lawyer phoned a district judge from the commissioner's office and, using the judge's first name, asked if something could be done. The attorney was told he would have to wait until court reconvened the following morning. Although the commissioner's decision for the time being was left standing, he still remarked afterward: "That's the kind of intimidation we commissioners have to put up with."

Police criticism, adverse publicity, and unpleasant encounters with citizens helped create an atmosphere of caution. But there were more direct sanctions heightening the risks facing the commissioners. During the first two years, three were removed from office. There were also five voluntary resignations, all by commissioners who worked the wearying midnight shift. The reason for removal in the three cases evidently was improper behavior, but it is instructive to consider the role of the police in one case and how some commissioners interpreted these removals.

Accused of being intoxicated while on duty, a commissioner was forced to resign. The accusation initially was made before the city comptroller's crime commission by a patrolman active in the FOP. He claimed the commissioner was so inebriated that bail hearings were delayed for five hours.[32] While most commissioners were reluctant to discuss the resignations, one felt they were the result of being "set up" by the police. In the instance of the commissioner accused of drinking on the job, he argued, only police officers were present during the incident. He added that the officer who made the accusation subsequently campaigned for the FOP presidency claiming, "I got a commissioner fired." Other commissioners also thought the resignations were due to police pressure, and one felt that because the head commissioner was a former detective, his superior did not ignore police complaints.

Working in a risk-laden environment in positions that afforded little protection from a variety of sanctions and threats, Baltimore's commissioners had few external incentives encouraging them to release felony defendants on minimal bails or their own recognizance. The risks accompanying bail choices for felony defendants, however, were exacerbated even further by the policies of the Pre-Trial Release Division. Indeed the problems or limitations the commissioners faced in using this administrative resource provide additional evidence for the commissioners' lament that they had responsibility but little power.

The Pre-Trial Release Division: A Reluctant Ally

Two policies of Baltimore's Pre-Trial Release Division limited its utility to commissioners when deciding whether to release a felony defendant on recognizance. First, according to the division's rules, a large proportion of felony defendants simply were not eligible for recognizance under its custody. Persons accused of murder, rape, armed robbery, narcotics offenses, kidnapping, abduction, arson, or assault on a police officer could not be recommended by its investigators for recognizance. This rule automatically excluded about 40 percent of the sample defendants. Secondly, unless there was a recommendation by one of its investigators, the agency would not supervise or be held responsible for any defendant who was granted recognizance by the commissioners. In effect, this meant that defendants charged with one of the excluded offenses would not be monitored by the agency if commissioners felt recognizance was warranted since they would not be recommended for this form of release in the first place. But the implications of this second policy extended even further to include other defendants in 1972. The division did not assign enough investigators to cover all the districts and shifts worked by the commissioners. Consequently, substantial numbers of defendants were not interviewed and hence no recommendations regarding recognizance could be made for those who were missed. During 1972–1973, for example, only about a quarter of all defendants, regardless of charge, were interviewed by a pretrial release investigator.[33]

These policies not only reduced the agency's usefulness to commissioners, they made the decision to free felony defendants on recognizance a considerably greater gamble for them. The commissioners had no guarantee that the felony defendants they released without an investigator's recommendation would be monitored or supervised by the agency's staff. They therefore were oftentimes singularly responsible for these decisions and their consequences, for unlike the Pre-Trial Release Division they lacked the organizational means of assuring the court appearance of defendants on whom they decided to take a chance or of monitoring their behavior before trial.

The policies of the Pre-Trial Release Division to some extent reflected the views of the Supreme Bench. The division's chief administrative aide, who had been with the organization from its start and who formulated most of its programs, stated during an interview that he felt the Supreme Bench as a whole was conservative, and this was an important factor behind the agency's policies. Indeed, these policies and the views of the Supreme Bench became a source of friction with the District Court. Attempts by the District Court's chief judge to get the Supreme Bench to change what he called the "asinine release rules" of the agency failed until the jail crisis in 1973 finally prompted the higher court to relax the agency's stance on excluded offenses and supervision of defendants. The chief judge stated, however, that he was unable to get it to "back away" from its position that the "defendant prove to them he should be released." Although the Pre-Trial Release Division did change its rules, it also ordered its investigators to mark all cases where defendants were released on recognizance without their recommendation as "specials" so that they would not be counted by the agency when it tallied its failure-to-appear rate.[34] Furthermore, although investigators were told that there were no longer any excluded offenses, they stated during the interviews that they were still reluctant to make recommendations for felony defendants.

PRISONER UNREST AND A LEGAL CHALLENGE: THE POLITICAL CRISIS OF BALTIMORE'S JAIL

Overlapping the first year of the commissioners' tenure in office was a series of incidents involving the Baltimore City Jail that ballooned into a full-fledged crisis for city and jail officials. Beginning with an inmate riot early in 1971 followed soon thereafter by the Legal Aid Bureau's lawsuit, the jail's troubles did not end until 1973. By then the Jail Board had been completely revamped, the warden had been fired, the mayor had announced the need to reduce the jail's population, and a new warden had been appointed. The jail case in federal court, concluded in 1972, did not place a cap on the facility's population and the mayor's decision was not made until 1973. Thus in 1972 the commissioners were free from the kind of resource constraint that figured so prominently in Detroit's policies. But this also meant that the political pressures on commissioners were not offset or counterbalanced by the need to hold the jail population down or to reduce it. Indeed, it will be suggested after reviewing Baltimore's jail crisis that even if they had been forced to take measures to do something about the jail's population, the capacity of the jail relative to the volume of felony defendants still would have permitted relatively stringent and costly policies.

In February 1971 a riot broke out in the jail's maximum security section following a fight between a jail guard and an inmate. During the riot "hundreds of windows were smashed, two guards were injured, and tear gas was used."[35] Prisoners later complained of bad food, inadequate medical care, poor living conditions, and abusive treatment. The Jail Board dismissed these charges as "without merit" soon afterward because "no formal grievances in writing as requested and as promised by the inmates at the time of the riot" had been received by the board.[36] Another major complaint by prisoners centered on court delays in hearing their cases. About one-third of the inmates had been awaiting trial for more than six months. The chief judge of the Supreme Bench was reported to have taken the position that any prisoners wanting an early trial only had to write the court and they would be tried promptly.[37]

Immediately after the riot the flamboyant and then politically popular warden took newspaper reporters and a television crew on a tour of the jail. Claiming it was a "model jail, one of the finest," he blamed the riot on a "bunch of Black Panthers who want to cause revolution in this country," and added, "We know through the censoring of mail this is strictly a national revolution."[38] Later, after the Legal Aid attorneys filed their case in court, he included them in his indictment as "ultra-liberals" and "store-front lawyers" for harassing him and fomenting jail unrest.[39] Significantly he maintained the jail easily could hold 1,900 prisoners; overcrowding had little to do with its problems according to the warden. At the time of the riot, the jail held approximately 1,600 inmates, roughly two-thirds of whom were awaiting trial in either District Court or the Criminal Court of the Supreme Bench.

In May the Legal Aid Bureau, prompted by prisoner complaints about the jail's conditions and particularly the disciplinary actions taken after the riot, entered their complaint in Federal District Court. The trial began the following January in 1972 and five months later the judge rendered his decision in favor of the complainants. In his written opinion, the judge bemoaned the rancor and hostility that had characterized the trial.

> I witnessed from the bench, displayed on the faces of witnesses and parties, the most deeply felt antagonisms and resentments. Nearly each time I made a ruling, even of a minor evidentiary nature, daggers of criticism, displeasure and deep emotion burst forth from the faces of the side against whom I ruled. And that was true of those in authority as well as those confined. . . . The tensions between those in command and those subject to command have long since passed the boiling point.[40]

Unlike the case in Detroit, the judge's ruling did not address overcrowding in Baltimore's jail. In an interview, the attorneys said they did not push the issue because the judge expressed doubts about federal judicial intervention in this area. At the same time, they felt the underlying reason was his apprehension over the political furor that, in their words, "closing down the jail" would have raised.[41] To some degree the attorneys representing the jail authorities played on these fears. In a posttrial brief, for example, they tried to distinguish the factual circumstances in

Baltimore from those in other jail cases (including Wayne County it might be noted) by stressing the extreme criminality of the jail's population. These cases, the attorneys argued,

> involved little county institutions, run by local sheriffs, or political hacks, located out in the boondocks, populated by only a few hundred inmates, most of whom were probably charged with stealing chickens from some farmer. Our case is entirely different. Here we have a large population (appr. 1,400) . . . with real diehard criminals, murders [sic], and rapists of the worst sort . . . . The Court should not lose sight of these salient facts in making its judgment in this matter and applying the law.[42]

Similarly, while stating he did not agree with "all aspects" of the defense position, the judge nonetheless quoted in his opinion its argument that defendants who failed to make bail were dangerous.[43]

> The fact that an inmate cannot raise bail set by the State Judiciary or is not bailable means that said inmate is considered by the law to be highly dangerous to persons and property, is a threat to society and should be incarcerated pending disposition of his trial, and that if the elaborate and presently exhaustive machinery of the State Judiciary does not consider a man a good risk for bail, then the Defendants, as prudent reasonable men, have a duty to act accordingly.[44]

The judge demurred, saying that detained defendants might be no more dangerous than those who made bail, the only difference being their financial resources. But this would be true, he concluded, "even under an effective and liberally administered pre-trial release agency."[45]

The question of bail and its effect on the jail's problems was not settled by the court.[46] Nor was the issue of court delay resolved. During the trial the administrative assistant of the State's Attorney Office testified that slightly more than 600 defendants were still in jail after more than four months awaiting trial in the Supreme Bench's Criminal Court and that about 475 defendants were in jail after a month or more waiting to have their cases heard in District Court.[47] Although the Legal Aid attorneys sought to have the federal court establish a maximum period for pre-trial detention, they later dropped this request. In part this was because the judge was persuaded the courts were taking steps to speed up their processes, and partly because he did not think it was within his jurisdiction.[48] The final decision, then, focused entirely on the constitutional violations posed by the jail's internal operations and policies.

Events both at the time of the trial and afterward, however, began to accumulate and propelled the crisis toward its conclusion. There were two more disturbances in the jail, one of which was minor in April 1972 and the other more serious in February 1973. The jail guards went on strike and staged a walkout during the summer of 1972 to press their demand that the warden resign because of allegedly making racist remarks. They also walked out after the February riot proclaiming they had received insufficient help from the police to quell the disorder. Shortly after the trial began the mayor, who had taken office in December 1971, asked the Federal Bureau of Prisons to inspect and evaluate the jail and its operations. This was quickly followed by the appointment of a commission headed by a prestigious local lawyer to investigate the jail after the April disturbance. Both reports were highly critical of the jail and warden which, combined with the federal court decision mandating changes in the jail, led the mayor to drastically alter the composition of the five-member Jail Board by appointing three new members and a new president. The warden was suspended for two weeks by the revamped board in August and finally fired in Spetember. By this time, which it is well to note was just a month or so after the first policeman was killed by a bailed defendant, the jail population had soared to nearly 1,800 persons, its highest mark in two years, as the commissioners tightened up their release decisions. The *Sun* declared a "RECORD EXCESS IN BALTIMORE JAIL" and described it as "bursting to its seams" with inmates "sleeping in its dayrooms and gymnasiums."[49]

In February 1973 the mayor announced the jail population would have to be reduced to 1,000 persons.[50] His decision partly was due to the pressure placed on him by a second commission appointed by him to assess the jail's medical facilities in September and by the federal judge's decree in December that the attorneys in the jail case meet with the Jail Board president to devise ways of reducing the jail's population. The meeting with aides from the mayor's office present was held in January but was not productive.[51] The jail, however, had also been a source of political embarrassment for the mayor. Early in his term he was reported to have been "more committed to battling 'crime in the streets' than solving jail problems."[52] But since then a source in City Hall, quoted by a reporter, said: "He has faced more embarrassment on jail problems than in any other area of government."[53] The mayor's decision was precipitated by the jail's third riot during which the *News-American's* front page proclaimed "INMATES CONTROL CITY JAIL."[54] At his news conference, the mayor stated the jail would continue to have problems "until the inmate population is trimmed to less than 1,000." But his ambivalence was indicated afterward when he "told several reporters that an outstanding warden and well-trained staff could handle 1,500 inmates."[55]

The mayor's decree did not specify how the jail population would be reduced. But in April, when the Supreme Bench approved a "high impact" program prepared by its Pre-Trial Release Division to reinterview felony defendants still detained after various bail reviews, it was greeted unenthusiastically. The *News-American*, for example, recognized that "reducing the population will eliminate or at least ameliorate the many problems with which the jail has been plagued in recent years." But it questioned whether reducing the scope of existing bail policies was appropriate. Conceding the magnitude of the jail's difficulties, the paper admitted "we are skeptical about this new program" and asked "is letting accused murderers or rapists go free on their own recognizance the best way to reduce the City Jail population? We think not."[56]

The commissioners did not report any conferences or discussions with the chief judge or administrative judge about the jail's problems. Indeed, when talking about the jail, the commissioners saw the issue as largely irrelevant to their decisions. Two commissioners voiced similar arguments; if they took the jail's difficulties into account it would "defeat the purpose" of being judicial officers with flexibility and autonomy in determining pretrial release conditions. In any case, they felt that they were not responsible for the jail's overcrowding. Other commissioners shared this view. Two amplified on it, however, by stating they assumed that if defendants were incarcerated it was probably because they were bad risks for the bondsmen if the bails were low, or there were good reasons for their detention if their bails were high. Another claimed that jailed defendants were "dredges" who did not deserve to be released. Besides, he added, if some defendants should have been released but somehow "slip through" at arraignments, he thought they would have their bails revised at later stages and ultimately be released.

During 1972, then, the commissioners were not forced to evaluate their pretrial release decisions in light of their possible impact on the jail. This is one difference compared to Detroit. Another equally important difference is that the capacity of the Baltimore jail relative to the volume of felony defendants arraigned annually in District Court provided the commissioners with greater detention resources than was the case in Detroit. This made more stringent pretrial release policies feasible in Baltimore.

The preceding discussion indicated the capacity of Baltimore's jail and whether it was overcrowded were matters of some debate. As late as 1969 a jail manual stated the facility could accommodate at least 2,000 prisoners. The warden after the first riot argued it could hold roughly 1,900 inmates with two prisoners in each of its 980 cells. The mayor's decision that it should house no more than 1,000 inmates was based on a study of the jail's medical facilities. The new warden, appointed in June 1973, reported that 1,150 to 1,250 persons could be incarcerated without undue difficulties.[57] During 1972, according to unpublished information from the warden's office, the average daily population was 1,351 although this masks wide fluctuations. Whether the jail was overpopulated ultimately was a political issue which, lacking an externally imposed definition as in Detroit, was influenced by events within the jail.

Regardless of which capacity figure is used, detention capabilities in Baltimore were sizable when compared to the number of felony defendants processed by the courts. Regrettably, official court data were neither adequate nor appropriate for this comparison since the clerk's office based its figures on charges, not defendants, and 54 percent of the sampled felony defendants had more than one charge lodged against them. The only information regarding the number of defendants was prepared by the State's Attorney Office for 1973.[58] While acknowledging that the number of defendants in 1972 undoubtedly was different, when this report's figure of 5,136 felony defendants is contrasted with either the high or low capacities of the jail, the facility provided ample space to detain a large proportion of these defendants pending trial.

District Court also handled misdemeanor defendants, however, and the 1973 total was estimated by the State's Attorney Office to be 31,742. While this number in combination with the felony volume would seem to dwarf the jail, the jail functioned primarily as a pretrial detention facility for felony defendants. Information for 1972 was not available, but data for nine days in April 1973, the closest month to 1972 of the data supplied by the warden's office, indicated that of an average daily population of 1,301 prisoners, a mean of 70 percent were awaiting trial and of these defendants 72 percent on the average were accused of assault, burglary, rape, robbery, or homicide according to the breakdown in the warden office's daily reports. In this sense, then, the relevant comparison is with the number of felony defendants.

It should also be recalled that there were many complaints about delays in the courts and the length of time defendants spent in jail before their cases were heard. This would suggest the turnover rate in the jail was probably lower than in Detroit and one result was a limiting effect on the jail's detention capabilities. Given the information that was available, it was not possible to fully explore this issue. Chapter 5, however, will show that detention rates were higher in Baltimore and the periods of incarceration longer than in Detroit. These outcomes were made possible in large part because of Baltimore's greater detention resources.

DEFINING BAIL REFORM IN AN ENVIRONMENT OF RISK

When the commissioners assumed their posts in District Court, they confronted a problem that did not exist in Detroit; the meaning of bail reform for persons accused of serious crimes had to be determined. The feasibility of liberalizing bail was limited by their political environment, but they were not constrained by scarce detention resources. In other words, their political environment raised the stakes of reducing bail conditions to minimal levels while the jail's detention capabilities did not hinder the imposition of stringent conditions for pretrial release. Within this zone, if they were to implement Rule 777 in a manner consistent with their obligations, they had to find the meaning of "nonexcessive" bail and decide whether security bonds were effective in guaranteeing the appearance of defendants. Rule 777 provided guidelines in these matters, but it was left to the commissioners to find specific rules of choice. As this final section of the chapter suggests, their solution emerged as a compromise between their responsibilities under Rule 777 and the risks and uncertainty they faced. The first part of this discussion focuses on the courtroom context of bail setting and how it fostered a cautious approach to the solution.

The Value of Caution in a Situational Context

The commissioners' definition of reform was both facilitated and hindered by conditions in the courtrooms where they worked. Their predispositions regarding the release of accused felons reflected a situational context in which light caseloads gave them time for their deliberations, and mixed dockets were an incentive to satisfy Rule 777 by releasing misdemeanor defendants. At the same time poor information aggravated the uncertainty of freeing felony defendants and bred a skeptical approach to their release. Only when commissioners negotiated with the police were the conditions fostering situational choices suspended, leading to a reduction in risk, a sharing of responsibility, and the release of a substantial portion of felony defendants.

The Work of Commissioners and Its Implications

The commissioners were assigned on a monthly rotating basis to the nine courtrooms located in the district police stations scattered about Baltimore. There were two eight-hour shifts beginning at 4:00 in the afternoon during the week and three shifts on weekends and holidays. They often worked alone and collected much of their own information. The courtrooms as a rule were deserted during bail hearings, except for the defendants, of course, who generally were brought in one at a time by the police turnkey for security reasons. Occasionally family members, relatives, or friends might be present, but defense attorneys and prosecutors were rare.

The proceedings tended to be relatively relaxed and informal, although this varied by commissioner as might be expected. Unlike Detroit where the judges in their black robes flanked by a retinue of court reporter, clerk, and arraignment officer lent bail hearings a certain formality (a formality given a second meaning by the quick and routine manner of the proceedings), the commissioners did not wear robes, and when it was warm, they worked in their shirtsleeves. Some eschewed the bench, preferring to use a desk off to the side, and one conducted hearings in chambers.

Also unlike Detroit, bail decisions unfolded in two distinct stages when the commissioners were working alone, and in three stages when

Pre-Trial Release investigators were present. Prior to the actual bail hearings the commissioners collected information, reviewed the files, and prepared summonses for witnesses. In the process of doing this they formed tentative conclusions about cases and developed ideas as to what they would do before seeing defendants. The hearings were a chance to test these conclusions against the appearance and behavior of defendants. When pretrial investigators were available, an earlier step preceded the normal process, namely interviewing defendants and verifying the interview information. All of this took time. Although the hearings ranged from 3 to 5 minutes to complete, not strikingly long even when compared to Detroit, the commissioners generally spent anywhere from 10 to 20 minutes working on a felony case prior to conducting the arraignment and bail hearing. The relatively light workloads of the commissioners facilitated this process.

Table 4.1 shows the average number of hearings for both warrant requests and bail by shift that were conducted by the commissioners during a two-week period in 1972. Compared to Detroit where the judges arraigned and set bail for 15 to 20 defendants within the span of an hour or so, Baltimore's officials were able to work at an unharried and relatively leisurely pace. During the evening shift the average number of hearings was 9.5 and for the midnight shift it was 6.5. Warrant requests, which based on observation and interviews with the commissioners normally involved marital and neighborhood disputes, accounted for about a third of the commissioners' workload, but were most frequent during the evening shift when the mean number of requests was 4.4 compared to 1.5 for the midnight shift. Bail hearings averaged about 5 per shift. Although workloads in the nine districts varied, ranging from a total mean of 5.5 to 14.1 hearings for the evening shift and from 4.5 to 8.3 for the midnight shift, it is clear the commissioners did not bear an onerous burden of cases during their eight hours of work.

TABLE 4.1   Average Workloads of Commissioners

Type of Hearing	Average Number of Hearings by Shift	
	Evening	Midnight
Warrant Request	4.4	1.5
	(N = 446)	(N = 150)
Bail Setting	5.1	5.0
	(N = 538)	(N = 563)
Average Number of Hearings	9.5	6.5
	(N = 984)	(N = 713)

SOURCE: Commissioner worklogs for August 21–September 3, 1972. Day shift on weekends excluded. Warrant requests also include citizen requests for arrest summonses.

The commissioners' worklogs did not indicate when bail hearings involved misdemeanor or felony charges. However, the State's Attorney Office's report on defendant volume indicates that felony cases were infrequent events for commissioners. Approximately 5,100 defendants out of a total of over 37,000 criminal defendants were accused of a felony crime in 1973. Dividing these numbers by the total number of shifts worked by the commissioners in a year (about 7,560) suggests that on the average the commissioners set bail for about one felony defendant out of every five criminal arraignments. Field observations substantiated the infrequency of felony cases.

Aside from the time light caseloads gave the commissioners to perform their tasks, the mixed character of the bail dockets had implications for how they viewed felony defendants. Against a backdrop of minor offenders, family quarrels, and neighborhood clashes, persons accused of burglary, distributing narcotics, or armed robbery were perceived as different. One commissioner drew the distinction succinctly when he referred to felony defendants as "criminals" and to misdemeanants as "mostly people." Being charged with a felony not only affected how defendants were viewed but the criteria used in assessing their backgrounds. Rule 777 stated that in establishing conditions for pretrial release commissioners were to consider the family ties and relationships of defendants, their employment status and history, financial resources, reputation, character or mental conditions, and length of residence in the community.

These characteristics were not defined. The commissioners had to supply the definitions, and the nature of the definitions varied according to the charge. For instance, one commissioner admitted he looked for "more stability" in felony cases. Another said that background and community considerations were "relative to the charge." Illustrating his point with a hypothetical example, he said that if the charge were armed robbery, the defendant had to live with his family, stay with them every night, show some kind of regular school attendance or employment, and have a member of his family or his minister in court in order to establish good community stability. Before considering a low bail when the charge was serious and the defendant had "any kind of record," the commissioner who distinguished between "criminals" and "people" asserted he wanted the family members in court during the bail hearings. Since a defendant's personal and community ties were supposed to be important criteria for choosing between recognizance releases and cash bail, the tendency among commissioners to tighten their standards by making them more exacting for felony defendants reduced their chances for recognizance release.

A second aspect of the mixed bail docket was the opportunity it provided commissioners to implement Rule 777 without incurring undue risks. In comparison to Detroit where judges had no alternative but to release felony defendants because of the limit placed on the jail's population, the commissioners could avoid freeing large numbers of these defendants on recognizance but still feel they were meeting their responsibilities by focusing on misdemeanor offenders. Moreover, the Pre-Trial Release Division was more likely to recommend and accept misdemeanants for recognizance which meant that the commissioners could diffuse some of the responsibility for these decisions. While data for 1972 were not available, the study commissioned by the District Court in 1973 indicated that 43 percent of the misdemeanants were freed on recognizance compared to 25 percent of the felony defendants.[59]

Such disparities are not unusual in criminal courts. The point here is that the tension between following a bail rule mandating recognizance release whenever possible and an environment fraught with risk could be relaxed because the large number of misdemeanor cases provided an ample supply of eligible candidates for recognizance. Their charges were minor and they met the less stringent criteria of community stability used for these charges. The commissioners could thus take a chance on them. This exposed them to less threat than if they freed felony defendants while allowing them to feel they were following the intent of Rule 777.

Information, Uncertainty, and the Role of Defendants

Deciding whom to release from custody and under what conditions is an inherently uncertain task. For Baltimore's commissioners it was made more difficult by the fact that the information needed for these decisions was often incomplete and unreliable. An even more basic problem regarding information existed, however. Except for those times when they were criticized because a defendant failed to appear or committed a crime while out on bail, they were rarely informed about the outcomes of cases. One commissioner described the problem he and other commissioners faced when he commented:

> You never know in this job how well you are doing! I would like to see what has happened in the cases . . . . I am really interested in knowing sometimes when it is a difficult case what has happened. You never get to know who has appeared and who hasn't.

Without this information, they could not easily adjust their decisions to what they learned about the actual behavior of defendants. Yet they perceived themselves, and were considered by others, as being responsible for these outcomes. This burden heightened their sensitivity to the uncertainty enveloping their work. As another commissioner explained, they were "hesitant" to release defendants because they "didn't know what would happen." Since they also were more likely to hear about their mistakes than about their successes, this bias in information may have been additional encouragement for exercising caution.

Much of the time the commissioners worked alone, and their isolation from other sources of information was not compensated by the quantity or quality of information at their disposal. Police documents provided minimal biographical data on defendants such as age, race, marital status, and occupation, and little more than the statutory language defining probable cause and the nature of the crime. The background information was frequently inaccurate because either defendants lied to the officers filling out the forms, or, particularly in the case of occupation, officers ignored fine distinctions and simply put down "laborer" or "self-employed" without further elaboration. And, if rushed to complete their paperwork, officers often skipped what was largely superfluous information of little value to them. The formal charge could be a misleading indication of the seriousness of the crime when, for example, the weapon in a robbery with a deadly weapon case turned out to be a pen knife and not a gun. For the commissioners this problem was compounded by the paucity of information contained in the statements on the arrest forms, which a commissioner described as "either so brief, vague, or both" that he could not rely on them. Thus the circumstances surrounding incidents were not known unless arresting officers or detectives came and talked to commissioners directly.

Adding further to their difficulties was the incompleteness and frequent unreliability of information regarding the criminal records of defendants. Commissioners did not have actual copies of these records. Instead they had to telephone central records of the police department where police cadets went through the department's file of arrest cards. Many times the cards if not incomplete were missing so the commissioners only learned whether the defendant's name was on record. At other times they found out the number of cards which gave them some notion as to the number of arrests but nothing more.

The aggravation and frustration voiced by commissioners when talking about these problems did not end there. Cadets often made mistakes and told commissioners that there was no record for a defendant or gave them information about the wrong person. As a consequence, commissioners complained of how frequently they were surprised to discover that defendants they thought were "clean" in fact had been arrested previously. For example, a commissioner related an incident when a cadet told him that a defendant to be arraigned for armed robbery had no record. Later during the bail hearing he was alarmed to find that the defendant not only had a prior armed robbery conviction but had another robbery case pending in court! This was not an isolated incident; other commissioners cited similar problems. One commissioner started recording the names of cadets who gave him information because he did not want to be responsible for their mistakes. Finally, there were times when commissioners, unable to learn whether defendants had prior records, had to bluff them to find out. A commissioner recalled, after a defendant denied he had a record, holding up a blank sheet of paper, pointing his pen at it, and asking him, "What about this...?" The defendant quickly interrupted him and proceeded to tell him about his record.

Lacking the kind of information that was routinely available in Detroit, the commissioners turned to defendants to fill in gaps or to substantiate weak or unverified information. As a consequence, defendants assumed an important role in shaping the context of choice. Their responses to questions, however, could not be accepted without a grain of salt. Commissioners were skeptical when listening to defendants, and, in varying degrees, the problem of uncertainty was left unresolved since acceptance of what defendants said ultimately rested on whether they could be trusted.

During the interviews, commissioners stressed the importance of seeing how defendants behaved during hearings. The hearings gave them a chance to "size up" defendants, to find out if they were "jail wise," to "read" them, to "figure them out," and to "pop" questions testing their honesty or character. The way defendants approached the bench, how they stood, whether they had their hands in their pockets, whether they avoided looking at the commissioner, or the manner in which they answered questions signaled whether they were respectful of the court, concerned over their situation, or showed signs of not being responsible for themselves. Oftentimes, as one commissioner stated, the "gut feelings" he developed about defendants prompted him to change his mind about what to do. Others said the hearings gave them the opportunity to get at the "intangibles" that objective information could not reveal. Once these intangibles were determined, the information in the files, according to another commissioner, was "something to hang your hat on," a way of justifying a decision.

In addition to assessing the demeanor of defendants, commissioners tended to probe, and, on occasion, challenge defendants. If a defendant had quit work, they asked, "Why'd you quit?" When a commissioner learned a defendant had left his part-time job at the YMCA without knowing beforehand whether he could find work elsewhere, he asked him about it. Another wanted to know why a defendant had stopped going to Alcoholics Anonymous four years earlier and why he was not seeking help currently. "Maybe you need it. You keep getting arrested. Why don't you see them?" he asked. When discrepancies arose, they cast doubt on the defendant's dependability. A commissioner expressed "great concern" after a defendant told him he had worked for seven years at the large social security complex in Baltimore since he knew from the pretrial release investigator that he had quit several months earlier. In another observed instance, a defendant claimed he did not use drugs. The commissioner promptly demanded to see his arms. Finding what he called a "railroad track," he berated the defendant, asking:

Don't you know better than to lie to a commissioner? Who are you trying to fool? Listen, if you don't tell the truth, you're going back there [the lock-up] until tomorrow and we'll try it again until you decide not to lie.

The commissioners felt that many defendants would try to put their best foot forward by shading the truth. One stated he had learned how to "go back and forth" to see if defendants were honest because "they try to manipulate the system." Commissioners discovered quickly, he added, that "everyone who comes in wants to get back on the streets," and to get out "they lie." Another commissioner thought drug addicts were least trustworthy. Pausing a moment, he then concluded:

But everyone lies! And you can't be sure who they will be! It's amazing how everyone on the streets, even if they never were arrested, knows about the system, and how they can use it to their advantage.

A third commissioner raised his eyebrows whenever defendants asked about recognizance or security bonds because, he said, it indicated they were "wise to the system." The commissioners were skeptical, then, when listening to defendants while at the same time trying to interpret what they heard so they could make a decision.

When pretrial investigators were present, they also played a part in assessing defendants during hearings. Because they had interviewed the defendants earlier, they alerted commissioners whenever differences and discrepancies cropped up between what they knew about the defendants and what the defendants said when questioned by the commissioners. One commissioner argued this was "probably the most valuable" aspect of having investigators in the courtroom; otherwise he had to "shoot from the hip" in assessing the honesty of defendants. Other commissioners voiced similar sentiments.

Aside from this, they felt the actual information gathered by investigators was largely redundant since they asked many of the same questions during the hearings. What they wanted were the impressions of defendants investigators developed through the interviews and particularly when they telephoned the references supplied by defendants to verify the information. In this way, commissioners were able to learn how the families or friends of defendants responded to their arrest. Whether they were surprised, angry, or nonchalant, were interpreted as signs of how seriously they viewed their relative's arrest, whether they had close relations, and whether they could be trusted to assume responsibility for release. The investigators also reported how the defendant behaved during the interview. Was he abusive or violent? Had he been evasive or cooperative? Did he seem in control of himself or was he taking drugs?

Trying to assess the defendants' characters took time, but it is problematic whether it assured commissioners that they were making the right choice. The uncertainty of these decisions, aggravated by poor and inadequate information and combined with skepticism about defendants, may have discouraged them from gambling too often on the release of accused felons. Thus the immediate, day-to-day conditions under which they worked may have produced a cautiousness that restrained their willingness to broaden too greatly the meaning of reform for felony defendants, wholly apart from their ability to do so given Baltimore's political climate.

One measure reflecting this cautiousness is provided by the sample data on subsequent changes in the commissioners' decisions. Approximately 30 percent of the sample defendants who were not released at arraignment had their bails subsequently changed, and, with the exception of only 5 of the 467 defendants involved, all the changes relaxed the pretrial conditions imposed by commissioners. About 20 percent of these changes involved defendants who had been remanded and later were granted either recognizance or cash bails. Nearly 22 percent received recognizance in place of their original cash bails, and 58 percent had their cash bail amounts reduced. In comparison only 14 percent of the defendants in Detroit had their bails changed after arraignment, but 19 percent of these changes involved the imposition of more demanding conditions for release. The commissioners, as will be suggested later, did lessen the stringency of the city's former bail practices. The amount of change, however, was a compromise between risk, uncertainty, and reform that in effect passed on a substantial share of the responsibility for releasing felony defendants to the District Court or Supreme Bench judges who reviewed the bails or heard the motions for bail reduction. This diffusion of responsibility was also exemplified when the commissioners negotiated with the police over the recognizance release of felony defendants.

Bargaining with the Police

Relations between the commissioners and police as might be expected were strained. If the police held little regard for the commissioners' work, this feeling was reciprocated by most commissioners who were just as critical of the police but lacked a forum like the FOP to their views. They frequently grumbled about "sloppy" police work, criticized police zealousness in arresting too many people for minor offenses, and angrily recalled the appearance of defendants after police "tried the case in the streets" as one commissioner phrased it. Considering this tense relationship, it is slightly surprising that of the relatively small proportion of felony defendants granted recognizance release 14 percent of them came about through the intercessions of the police. In other words, about one out of seven defendants freed on recognizance by commissioners were at police request.

Clearly these requests posed high risks for commissioners. The police had not hesitated to accuse them of incompetence or of endangering the city's safety by releasing defendants with lengthy records. Moreover, these decisions were personally repugnant to commissioners because the defendant, usually a narcotics informant, was seen as "so awful that I wouldn't want him to touch me," as one commissioner stated. Another felt informers became so accustomed to receiving favors from the police that they were not especially dependable.

Why, then, despite the risk and personal reservations, did commissioners go along with the police? The answer can be found in the conditions imposed by commissioners when they cooperated with the police which greatly reduced the liabilities normally attached to this choice. When the police wanted a defendant released, the commissioners demanded that they sign a note stating they had asked for the bail. If they refused, the request was denied. On the other hand, if they agreed, the note was placed in the file as protection for the commissioners. The major factor behind this willingness to accede to police requests was the fact that commissioners reported their superiors did not sanction them for these decisions or for the actions of defendants released in this manner.

A commissioner talked about an instance when the police wanted a defendant charged with narcotics distribution freed on recognizance. He said he wanted a note from the police before he would go along. Soon after he got a letter from a high-ranking officer and the commissioner said he put it in the file. When the defendant didn't appear in court, the commissioner said he was put on the spot. What had happened was that a clerk had taken the letter out of the file because he didn't want the District Court judge to see it. By chance the commissioner said he found it and placed it in a safe place. So when the head commissioner phoned him and demanded that he better be able to explain what he had done, he told him about the letter. The head commissioner ordered him to get the letter to the administrative judge "pronto". He did, and he didn't hear anymore about it.

What about police demands for high bails? Unfortunately, no direct evidence on this question was available. One commissioner said such requests were infrequent; the police usually contacted him about recognizance releases. Another claimed that it was more frequent. "It goes on all the time," he reported. Whatever the frequency with which they were approached by police, commissioners unanimously denied they followed these requests. When they were made, they were seen as police "pressure" and an infringement on commissioner autonomy and authority. According to one commissioner his typical reaction to requests for high bail was, "If a cop comes in and says, 'This is a bad guy. Lock him up and throw away the key,' then you say, 'Thanks,' and do what you think is right in the case." While phrased in varying ways by his colleagues, this statement was echoed by other commissioners.

It would be rather naive to think the police, knowing the commissioners' feelings about such requests, did not try to persuade them in less direct ways to gain the same ends. The paucity of good information during bail hearings was discussed earlier. It is possible arresting officers or detectives exploited this opportunity by giving commissioners more information about a case than normally was available in hopes of getting a higher bail. Although Baltimore's police chief had ordered his officers not to talk to commissioners about cases or about bail, obviously requests for special treatment of narcotics informants were made rather often. There is no reason, then, to expect that officers did not try to shape commissioners' decisions in other instances, especially when the charges were serious. Unfortunately, data on this issue were not available, unlike the case of requests for recognizance.

Nevertheless, the commissioners said their reactions to police requests for high bails differed from those for recognizance. Taking them at their word that explicit requests for higher bails were denied while requests for recognizance or low bails were granted, an explanation for this difference may stem from the commissioners' norms regarding bail and how they viewed their roles. Although commissioners often expressed reservations about Rule 777's intent, they still saw themselves as responsible for assuring the defendant's right to nonexcessive bail, if not recognizance release, and police requests for high bail violated this view. Furthermore, to have gone along with these requests would have meant a return to the discredited police-court team and a diminution of their authority. Police requests for recognizance, however, did not violate these views. The police assumed responsibility for a defendant's release and they did so under conditions established by the commissioners. If they refused to agree to these conditions by not signing the note, the commissioners still retained their authority to set bail. Finally, it is important given the commissioners' vulnerability that they did not expect to be sanctioned by their superiors if they agreed to the requests. The risks inherent in these decisions thus were absorbed by the police and by the court's higher ranking judges.

Searching for Guidance: Formal and Informal Rules of Choice

While the factors shaping the bail setting context influenced the decisional predispositions of commissioners, generally steering them away from recognizance unless there was an agreement with the police, there still remains the issue of how bail amounts and type of bail were determined. At this point, then, the focus shifts to the cues commissioners used in establishing the bail tariff in 1972. Although the particular factors varied somewhat, the common denominator, once again, was the balance they sought between risk and reform. In the case of bail amounts the practices of the old Municipal Court lingered on as an influence on the commissioners as did the reactions of judges to their decisions. As for security bonds, Rule 777 was rarely followed because of the issue of who would be responsible for the behavior of defendants.

"Reasonable Bail:" The Past as Prologue and Following the Judges

The worrisome and seemingly insoluble problem of money bail, whether surety or security, is deciding the amount. How much should it be? Why require X amount rather than Y? At issue is the meaning of "nonexcessive" bail. In coming to the lower bench the commissioners immediately and abruptly had to come to grips with this problem, especially since they decided that three-quarters of the defendants they arraigned required cash bails.

It was difficult for them to offer precise definitions of excessive bail. As one complained, "No one has ever sat down to give an explanation as to what bail should be or what 'excessive' might be." On the other hand, they felt that they knew when bail was too low. For example, another commissioner argued, "If I set a bail for $100 on a defendant with a robbery charge, he's going to say to himself that $100 is a cheap price to pay to avoid 20 years." But at what point bail became excessive as opposed to lenient was not quite so clear to them, and under some circumstances they knew bail might be excessive even at minimal levels. It depended partly on the nature of the charge, of course, as this commissioner's comments just suggested, but also on the defendant's particular situation. A bail of "even $5," one commissioner remarked, might be too much if the defendant were indigent. How then did the commissioners settle on cash bails that would attain the goals of the new bail system while not being too lenient? Their solution drew partly on what they were able to learn about District Court judges and their preferences, but another important guide was simply their knowledge of the Municipal Court's bail schedule and how bails had been determined in the past. This knowledge helped establish a criterion for excessive bail and thus a benchmark to judge what bail amounts would satisfy the reform aspirations of Rule 777.

Before the inauguration of District Court most commissioners had worked as police officers or as investigators for the Pre-Trial Release Division. Through these work experiences they had become familiar with the bail amounts set by the police in Municipal Court. Furthermore, copies of the old bail schedule still could be found two years after the court's demise. None of the commissioners was observed using the schedule; Rule 777 expressly forbade its use. Nonetheless, the pervasiveness of these older bail amounts showed up repeatedly. A commissioner, who had been a pretrial release investigator, after deciding to require a cash bail for a misdemeanor nonsupport charge, was seen setting a cash amount equal to the old bail schedule. A retired patrolman reported the "normal" amount for a burglary charge was $3,500—the amount in the schedule for residential daytime burglaries. A third commissioner with no prior experience in the courts or any related agencies was asked if he had any initial bail amounts in mind when making his decisions. He replied that for armed robbery he used $10,000 and for nighttime burglary $5,000. Each of these amounts was specified in the bail schedule.

Commissioners appointed after 1971 were trained by seasoned commissioners and learned these bail amounts from them. One who had been in his position for about six months at the time of the interview had no previous experience in criminal courts. He stated that the commissioner who trained him taught him what bail amounts to use. Another commissioner, a part-time law student, said he made "copious notes" during his training period and later when he was on his own he said he checked them to see what his mentor had done. Still he could not help but wonder "how do you know what _____ was doing right?"

This commissioner's uncertainty was shared by others and led many of them to check the court dockets to see what judges did in cases when there was a bail review. The dockets (and law books it might be noted) were infrequently accessible to commissioners, however, because the court clerks fearing they might be stolen or lost put them in locked cabinets, and the commissioners were not given duplicate keys. Still, on occasion, they did learn that their decisions had been changed, and they reported they adopted the judge's decision as a guideline for subsequent cases. For example, a commissioner recalled there were several charges against a defendant for distributing narcotics and he put a bail of $2,500 on each of them. Later on he was able to check the bail review and found that the court's administrative judge had increased the amounts to $5,000 a charge. While he did not agree with the change, the commissioner appreciated the judge's decision since as he put it such cases were "politically sensitive." Consequently, he adopted the $5,000 amount as a benchmark when dealing with these kinds of cases.

The study of Rule 777 done in 1973 for the District Court also found commissioners took their cues from judges. In a footnote the study stated:

> ...one commissioner commented that a judge in his district believes that shoplifters should never be released except on high money bail. Commissioners in that district therefore set high money bail for shoplifters. By contrast, a commissioner in another district mentioned shoplifting as one of the charges which usually gets an arrestee a release on personal recognizance. Similar comments were made by other commissioners about their perceptions of what a particular judge wanted done with a particular type of offender.

The prior work experience of commissioners, their training, discussions with other commissioners, and checking the decisions or reactions of judges all provided bits and pieces to the puzzle as to what bail amounts should be. The tendency for commissioners to have bail amounts in mind for particular charges does not mean they were imposed in every case, however. Instead, the amounts were a starting point, a "ball park" figure, in the decision process that made the problem of determining bail amounts more manageable. Commissioners began with a particular amount and then adjusted this initial amount as they learned more about the defendant and the case.

Table 4.2 compares the median bail amounts in 1972 with the amounts for various charges in the former bail schedule. Because the charge variable for the sample data is a composite of individual charges, comparisons between the bail amounts for each charge are not exact. The data in Table 4.2 therefore should be treated as suggestive. The 1968 bail schedule did not include any amounts for narcotics charges (which may explain why the commissioner adopted the administrative judge's revision as a guide), and rape and murder charges were "no bails" or remands. The median cash bails set by the commissioners were lower than those on the bail schedule. Reform of Baltimore's lower court bail rules evidently did reduce the potential cost of pretrial punishment for felony defendants. By the same token, it is well to recall that bail amounts in Detroit were much lower than those set in Baltimore, both before and after reform.

The commissioners apparently discounted the bail amounts that had been typical of Municipal Court. They frequently mentioned that "bail should not be punishment" and in large measure what they defined as punishing bail may have been determined by the Municipal Court bail

TABLE 4.2 A Comparison Between the 1968 Bail Schedule and Cash Bails Set in 1972

Charge	Amount on 1968 Bail Schedule	Median Cash Bails in 1972
Larcency over $100 (theft)	$ 2,500	$1,500
Burglary		(N=85)
Dwelling: night	$ 5,000	
Dwelling: day	$ 3,500	$3,000
Other premises	$ 3,000	(N=312)
Robbery		
Not armed	$ 7,500	$5,000
		(N=184)
Armed	$10,000	$8,000
		(N=241)
Assault		
With intent to rape	No bail	
Carnal knowledge	$ 5,000	
With intent to murder	$ 7,500	$7,000
With intent to rob	$ 5,000	(N=43)
With intent to maim	$ 3,500	

schedule. There was another facet to this view, however. Municipal Court's bail schedule had no provision for recognizance release for felony defendants and no consideration for mitigating circumstances. Accordingly, they may have assumed that their bails were not excessive as long as they considered other factors than just the formal charge and if their bails were generally lower than those on the bail schedule. From this perspective it becomes clearer why a high rate of recognizance releases was not necessary as a measure of success for Baltimore's reforms. With a history of nondiscretionary high cash bails behind them, the commissioners by discounting these amounts could feel the goals of reform were being fulfilled since defendants were receiving lower bails than had been typical in Baltimore's previous lower court. Failure to make bail and gain release from jail were not indications of unreasonable bail, however. As the comments of commissioners indicated earlier, if bondsmen would not take defendants as customers, they implicitly confirmed their judgment that the defendants were not good risks.

Looking for Security: The Preference for Surety Bonds

Commissioners could reduce the loss of income suffered by defendants when cash bails were imposed if security bonds were chosen rather than surety bonds. Security bonds allow defendants to post a certain percentage, usually 10 percent, of the bail amount with the court. This deposit is then returned to them after the disposition of their cases as long as they have appeared for all the proceedings. In contrast, with surety bonds, defendants are forced to pay nonrefundable premiums to bondsmen for their release. As a means of controlling the behavior of defendants, security bonds rest on the threat of criminal penalties for willful failure to appear for a trial or hearing, the loss of the deposit placed with the court, and the potential loss of additional money if the court sues them for the balance of the bond. With surety bonds, bondsmen are the principal means of controlling defendants. They have the authority to arrest defendants and can place liens on their property for the balance of the surety bond if there is a bail forfeiture.

Rule 777 explicitly empowered Baltimore's commissioners to use security bonds. Moreover, it stated that security bonds were to be considered before sureties if commissioners thought recognizance releases would not be effective in assuring the trial appearance of defendants. Despite the rule's injunctions, commissioners did not view security bonds as an alternative to surety bonds and used it rarely; only about 8 percent of the cash bails in the sample involved security bonds. They gave two reasons for this preference.

First, Rule 777 laid out a ladder of alternative forms of restraint with securities on a lower rung than sureties. When commissioners juxtaposed this ladder against the scale of charges, they felt securities did not provide them with sufficient leverage over defendants accused of felony crimes. One commissioner said securities were useful if he needed a "little extra" to keep a defendant in the city and the charge was "moderate" and the defendant had a "pretty good record." A second commissioner expressed similar thoughts, securities were useful when there was "some doubt about the defendant but not much." Another viewed securities as "just a step removed from recognizance" and concluded that the defendant might just as well be put on recognizance.

An observed example of an instance when a commissioner employed a security bond occurred in a case where the defendant was charged with a misdemeanor offense of possessing marijuana.

There was some question as to the age of the young black defendant. He said he was seventeen, but the police had recorded his age as eighteen. Whether the defendant was eighteen or seventeen was important, as it determined which court, District or Juvenile, had jurisdiction over the defendant. The defendant steadfastly maintained he was seventeen, but could not provide official documentation of his birthdate. The only reference he gave the pretrial investigator was his grandmother. When she was telephoned, she was not able to give a firm answer and the investigator said she didn't seem "strong" about her grandson, i.e., she didn't appear to be favorably disposed toward him. During the hearing the commissioner said he thought the defendant's coloring was bad, and it seemed to him the defendant used drugs. Furthermore, the defendant was evasive and didn't look directly at the commissioner when he was questioned. The pretrial investigator declined to accept the defendant for recognizance. The commissioner decided to set a security bond of $250 with 10 percent which meant the defendant would have to deposit $25 to gain his release.

Related to the perceived proximity of security bonds to recognizance releases as a form of restraint was the opinion that in most instances the defendant was not the person who would make the deposit. Consequently, as one commissioner argued, security bonds did not "make an impression" on defendants because, if they failed to appear, they would not suffer the monetary penalty for their behavior. In order to make this sanction credible and immediate, he said he looked for "someone who is very close to the defendant" so that if he did not appear, this person would lose the security deposit.

The absence of a third party who could be held accountable for the defendant's appearance was the second major reason why security bonds were chosen infrequently. For recognizance release the pretrial release organization generally was supposed to be responsible for the defendant. With surety bonds it was the bondsman. But, if security bonds were selected, commissioners felt there was no intermediary who could be held to account for the behavior of defendants. The commissioners, therefore, did not consider security bonds an effective means of controlling defendants. They understood, as one phrased it, that surety bonds were like "throwing money down the phone wire" for defendants because bondsmen had to be paid for their services. Nevertheless, they were seen as an effective means of bringing defendants to court. With these views regarding the relative merits of security and surety bonds, the commissioners preferred to use securities sparingly and only for defendants who were otherwise marginal recognizance releases.[60]

CONCLUSIONS: TOWARD A MODEL OF POLICY SEARCH

As Machiavelli's warning foretold, implementing Maryland's liberal bail rule in Baltimore was a difficult, perilous, and uncertain venture for the District Court commissioners. Prodefendant sentiment was weak, and support for narrowing the scope of pretrial punishment for felony defendants lacking. The commissioners' positions exposed them to the threat of sanctions and gave them little protection. Their vulnerability and the uncertainty surrounding the decision process, which was exacerbated by inadequate and unreliable information, discouraged them from experimenting freely with the release of felony defendants on their own recognizance. And buttressing these disincentives were the policies of the Pre-Trial Release Division. On the other hand the commissioners were not constrained by scarce detention resources. Under these conditions, then, surety bonds were not only politically tolerable, but institutionally feasible, and from the commissioners' perspective more effective than security bonds. Under Rule 777, however, they were charged with effecting changes in the city's bail tariff. For most felony defendants, these changes involved discounting the bail amounts that would have been imposed under the old Municipal Court bail schedule. Bail-setting policies in Baltimore during 1972, therefore, reflected the commissioners' search for a secure path between the risks of reform and their responsibilities under Rule 777.

At the end of the chapter on Detroit, a political choice model of policy change was presented that depicted the conditions and sequence of steps leading to the adoption of various policy options affecting the scope and cost of pretrial punishment. This model, it will be recalled, focused on the response of criminal courts to overcrowding in local jails, and when different policies would be instituted to cope with this problem depending on the degree of political concern and the amount of slack that existed in the courts' disposition procedures. The rule governing these choices was based on minimizing the risks associated with options aimed at alleviating the jail's difficulties. Accordingly, the model posited that policies accelerating the outflow of jailed defendants, the "speedy trial" option, would be preferred over bail policy changes reducing the influx or inflow of defendants into the jail. In concluding this chapter, it would be useful to reevaluate this model in light of the events and circumstances in Baltimore.

Because the model drew on Detroit's experiences, the processes it outlined began with the issue of overcrowding and whether it sparked political concern. But in Baltimore events evolved differently, and these differences highlight the pivotal importance of an earlier stage that must occur before jails begin to play a major role in shaping policy changes in courts. Essentially this issue boils down to whether jail problems, such as riots, escapes, prisoner grievances, etc., are interpreted by key political actors as more or less the direct consequence of overcrowding and whether reducing the jail's population is an acceptable remedy. If other causes such as the jail authority's management policies are viewed as the reasons for current problems, attention naturally will turn to these policies thereby steering concern away from court practices.[61]

Defining the jail's problems in terms of overcrowding ultimately is influenced greatly by political considerations. In Baltimore the federal judge made it known to the Legal Aid attorneys that he would not establish and place a limit on the size of the population that could be incarcerated in the city's jail. Nor was he willing to deal with the question of court delay that undoubtedly helped produce a higher inmate population than would have been the case had Baltimore's courts moved more swiftly. Events involving the jail, of course, pushed the issue of overcrowding to center stage, forcing the mayor to conclude, albeit reluctantly, that its population would have to be reduced.

Unlike Detroit where Recorders' Court had identified overcrowding as a problem even before the court case put a population cap on the jail, Baltimore came to this position slowly. Concern over what would happen by "closing down the jail" had to be counterbalanced by the political embarrassment caused by its problems before the jail issue eventually was translated into an overcrowding problem. In addition two other factors deserve notice. For one thing general acceptance of earlier, larger capacity figures and the fact that later estimates were so much smaller (along with the implications that accepting them might entail) may have worked against and slowed down acceptance of overcrowding as a problem needing a solution. Another and related reason may be that it was not readily apparent to the actors, and more likely there was disagreement among them, regarding the respective contributions that the warden's policies, court delays, and overcrowding made to the jail crisis.

Once overcrowding was accepted as requiring attention in Baltimore, the policy response was somewhat similar to what the political choice model would have predicted. For example, the Supreme Bench announced in July 1973 that it would expand its criminal bench by adding two more courtrooms to expedite trials in serious criminal cases.[62] In other words the policy adjustment to the mayor's decision was to speed up the tempo of dispositions to help reduce the jail's population. In one respect, however, the response in Baltimore differed from the model which indicated that using bail reviews to release jailed defendants would follow such speedy trial efforts if they failed to produce the population reductions needed. Shortly after the mayor's decisions, it will be remembered, the Pre-Trial Release Division instituted its "high impact" program to reassess the status of jailed felony defendants to see if they could be released. Although this response came earlier than the model indicates, it is important to note it focused on the "outflow" side of the jail

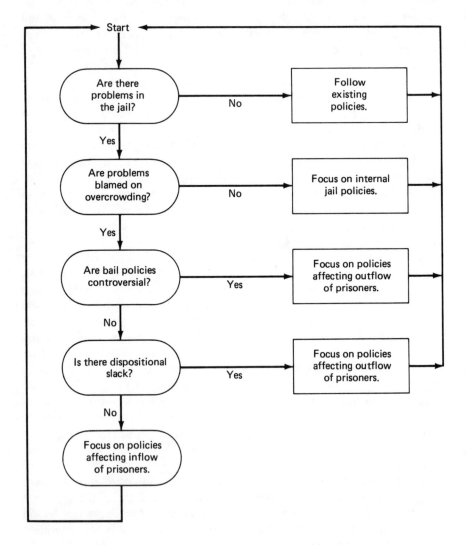

FIGURE 4.1 A Political Choice Model of Policy Search.

population equation affecting turnover in the jail and not on the arraignment stage where the flow of defendants into the jail originates.[63]

This deviation from the original model introduces a second neglected consideration affecting the process of policy change, namely, the extent to which bail policies are controversial. At this point it should be abundantly clear that bail in Baltimore was the center of considerable conflict. Further elaboration hopefully is unnecessary, but the important implication of this battle is that it probably ruled out serious consideration of drastically contracting the scope of bail policies at the arraignment stage. This conflict, then, made it improbable that the commissioners would be directed to orient their bail decisions in ways that would have paralleled those in Detroit's court. As a result, remedies for the jail focused on the outflow of defendants and, despite the changes made by the commissioners, bail setting in Baltimore was more restrictive than in Detroit.

To conclude this chapter these lessons from Baltimore have been incorporated into a model of policy *search* as shown in Figure 4.1. Rather than a detailed decision model as shown earlier in Figure 3.6, the emphasis in this second model is more general, and, as the title suggests, it is intended to portray the basic conditions and policy areas where search will be undertaken for solutions to problems stemming from the jail. This model leaves open the exact nature of the options that will be chosen. Instead it suggests that depending on how jail problems are diagnosed, whether initial bail policies are controversial, and whether dispositional slack exists, antidotes to the jail's maladies will be sought in those areas either nearest the problem—as when jail issues are defined as internally generated—or in those areas affecting one of the two parts of the jail population equation. This model still retains, however, the underlying premise that the process of search is governed by the risk minimization rule. Consequently, only if the conditions in a city match those represented by the sequence shown on the left side of the model will attention be focused on finding ways of minimizing the scope and cost of punishment before trial.

REFERENCES

1. Peter Bachrach and Morton S. Baratz, *Power and Poverty*, New York, Oxford University Press, 1970, p. 69.
2. Ibid., p. 79.
3. See *Report of Baltimore Committee on the Administration of Justice under Emergency Conditions*, Baltimore, Md. 1968. Perhaps the fact that Baltimore's riot was neither unexpected nor isolated (many cities had similar disturbances after the assassination) diffused the apparent need to look more critically at the city's courts.
4. See Bachrach and Baratz, *Power and Poverty*, pp. 116–117 for brief descrip-

tions of the districts in the mid-sixties. In 1973 a long-time councilman from the first district complained after several gubernatorial appointments to fill vacancies in District Court that his district was being slighted. The Baltimore *Sun* editorially concurred with this complaint, stating that "the present make-up of the court leaves it without a semblance of desirable geographic balance." See Baltimore *Sun*, July 20, 1973.

5. Ernest Patterson, *Black City Politics*, New York, Dodd, Mead and Company, 1975, p. 256.
6. James Eisenstein and Herbert Jacob, *Felony Justice*, Boston, Little, Brown and Company, 1977, p. 92.
7. *Collins v. Schoonfield*, 344 F. Supp. 257, 1972.
8. Eisenstein and Jacob, *Felony Justice*, p. 92.
9. Baltimore *Sun*, December 11, 1972.
10. Ibid., February 28, 1973.
11. This brief history draws heavily from the section on Baltimore's courts in the President's Commission on Law Enforcement and Administration of Justice, *Task Force Report: The Courts*, Washington, D.C., U.S. Government Printing Office, 1967, pp. 121–128.
12. In 1972 all of the judges in District Court had been "grandfathered" in from Municipal Court and with the exception of two all were being investigated for participating in the traffic-ticket scandal.
13. President's Commission, *Task Force Report*, p. 123.
14. Ibid., p. 123.
15. *Baltimore News-American*, September 25, 1972.
16. Baltimore *Evening Sun*, September 29, 1971.
17. Baltimore *Sun*, January 17, 1972.
18. Ibid., August 4, 1972.
19. Ibid., September 22, 1972.
20. *Baltimore News-American*, September 24, 1972.
21. Ibid., September 27, 1972.
22. Ibid., September 25, 1972.
23. Ibid.
24. Ibid., September 24, 1972.
25. Ibid., April 12, 1973.
26. Ibid., January 18, 1973.
27. Baltimore *Evening Sun*, January 23, 1973.
28. *Baltimore News-American*, January 21, 1973.
29. National Council on Crime and Delinquency, *Pretrial Release in Maryland: A Study of Maryland District Rule 777*, Hackensack, N.J., 1974.
30. *Baltimore News-American*, April 13, 1973.
31. Baltimore *Sun*, March 4, 1973.
32. Baltimore *Sun*, April 11, 1973.
33. This is at best an estimate. According to a State's Attorney Office report approximately 37,000 misdemeanor and felony defendants were processed in District Court during 1973. The Pre-Trial Release Division reported it interviewed 8,258 defendants in 1972 and 9,624 in 1973. See Baltimore State's Attorney Office, "Yearly Activity Report—1973—District Court," Baltimore, Md., 1974 (mimeographed); and Pre-Trial Release Division, *Fifth Annual Report*, Baltimore, Md., 1973.

34. The division had great pride in its low failure-to-appear rate, which its annual report stated was less than 1 percent of the defendants released in its custody. This was considerably lower than the rates in the cities Wice studied which ranged from 2.3 to 19.0 percent, see Paul Wice, *Freedom for Sale*, Lexington, Mass., Lexington Books, 1974. One way the agency was able to produce such a low rate was by "rescinding" defendants. In the event defendants neglected to maintain regular contact with the division, the agency went to the Supreme Bench and had a warrant issued for their arrest. This procedure was followed regardless of whether defendants actually failed to appear in court and removed them from the division's custody. According to unpublished data compiled by the division, 1,095 persons were rescinded between 1968 and 1974, about 5 percent of the defendants released under its supervision. By focusing so intently on its failure-to-appear rate the agency essentially was willing to accept a lower overall rate of recognizance, a priority underlying its other policies.
35. Baltimore *Sun*, 20, 1971.
36. Ibid.
37. Ibid., February 28, 1971.
38. Ibid., February 20, 1971.
39. Baltimore *Evening Sun*, August 6, 1971.
40. *Collins v. Schoonfield*, p. 268.
41. Perhaps because of the jail's extreme overcrowding in September the court's second interim decree issued in December urged officials to meet to see what could be done to reduce the jail's population. The court did not set a maximum population, however. See M. Kay Harris and Dudley P. Spiller, Jr., *After Decision: Implementation of Judicial Decrees in Correctional Settings*, Washington, D.C., U.S. Government Printing Office, 1977, for a thorough study of the *Collins v. Schoonfield* case.
42. Harris and Spiller, *After Decision*, p. 421.
43. The attorneys for the inmates had raised the issue that indigent defendants were detained because they could not make bail, see Plaintiff's Brief, *Collins v. Schoonfield*, p. 12.
44. *Collins v. Schoonfield*, p. 284.
45. Ibid., p. 284.
46. The Wayne County Circuit Court also refused to make a ruling on the issues raised about bail by the plaintiff's attorneys, see *Wayne County Jail Inmates v. Wayne County Board of Commissioners*, Civil Action 173 217, Circuit Court for the County of Wayne, Mich., 1971, pp. 74–75.
47. Baltimore *Sun*, February 2, 1972.
48. *Collins v. Schoonfield*, p. 284.
49. Baltimore *Sun*, September 4, 1972. Since they were additional evidence of the jail's failings, it bears mentioning that over the course of the crisis, there were 38 escapes, 3 murders or suicides, and 14 assaults or homosexual rapes of inmates reported in the newspapers.
50. *Baltimore News-American*, February 27, 1972.
51. Harris and Spiller, *After Decision*, p. 379.
52. Baltimore *Sun*, April 2, 1972.
53. *Baltimore News-American*, February 27, 1973.
54. Ibid., February 25, 1973.

55. Ibid., February 27, 1973.
56. Ibid., April 22, 1973.
57. Harris and Spiller, *After Decision*, p. 387.
58. Baltimore State's Attorney Office, "Yearly Activity Report."
59. National Council on Crime and Delinquency, *Pretrial Release*, Table 8, p. 3.18. It should be noted the percentages given in the text were recalculated by dropping those cases with no data and by combining the two misdemeanor categories presented in the report's table. Also the percentages reflect the *final* release status of defendants, not the type of bail at the time of arraignment which means that the percentages for the initial stage of the process probably were lower.
60. Another reason for the commissioners' reluctance to use security bonds may have been the fact that one of the commissioners who was forced out of office was indicted for malfeasance and obtaining money under false pretenses. He was accused of pocketing a security bond deposit; see Baltimore *Sun*, February 9, 1973. One commissioner during an interview mentioned that he had difficulty allaying police suspicions that he and the other commissioners were doing the same thing.
61. Another alternative is to attribute the jail's difficulties to the inmates, a tack taken by Baltimore's warden when he blamed Black Panthers for the first riot. If Legal Aid had not filed its complaint, this effort might have been successful and the warden's policies would not have come under attack.
62. An earlier response occurred in 1972 when the chief judge of the Supreme Bench assumed authority to limit postponements in criminal cases in an effort to cut delays. While no data were available on the impact of this effort, Chapter 5 shows disposition times in Baltimore were quite long. See also Eisenstein and Jacob, *Felony Justice*, pp. 256–257, for a brief discussion of this issue. In passing it might also be noted that earlier attempts to quicken the pace in the Supreme Bench based on controlling postponements had failed; see Baltimore *Sun*, July 2, 1969 and September 26, 1969. Shortly after this the Supreme Bench added three courtrooms bringing the total to eight during 1972. Again it is relevant that these actions were prompted by a hunger strike and demonstrations by inmates in the jail.
63. It will be recalled that the division also eliminated, at least formally, its "excluded offense rule" and agreed to make bail, *not* recognizance, recommendations for these defendants after a meeting with the District Court's chief judge. It was because of these changes that some investigators carried copies of the old bail schedule in the event they were asked to make recommendations as to bail amounts by commissioners. But observations of hearings after 1972 when investigators were more often present still indicated that they rarely made recommendations other than those pertaining to recognizance.

5

Policy Outcomes and the Political Economy of Surety Markets

INTRODUCTION

The central concern of the last two chapters has been to explain why the bail setting policies of Detroit and Baltimore differed. Guided by the organizational perspective developed in Chapter 2, the focus of the two case studies concentrated on the contexts and characteristics of the decision processes that influenced and shaped the choice behavior of the officials who decided the pretrial release conditions of felony defendants. In both cities the policies manifested how the courts and their officials resolved the conflicting responsibilities, expectations, and demands impinging on them. But because these conditions differed, so did their resolution, and hence, the scope and cost of pretrial sanctions in the two cities. Detroit's judges chose recognizance release much more frequently than Baltimore's commissioners and the bail amounts they imposed were less onerous. There is one more question that needs to be answered. Did the outcomes of these policies match their potential punitiveness? More specifically, were release rates and the costs borne by defendants consistent with what might be expected given the differences in scope and bail amounts in the two cities?

At first blush the issue seems trite and the answer obvious. With nearly half of the sampled defendants in Detroit freed on their own recognizance and the other half required to post relatively small surety bonds, outcomes for defendants would be less punishing than in Baltimore where most defendants had to post cash bails of substantially higher amounts. And so they were, as will be seen shortly. But there are two major reasons for being a bit more skeptical about the outcomes of bail setting policies, even when they are as different as Detroit's and Baltimore's were in 1972.

For one thing the extent of pretrial sanctioning is not solely determined by the decisions made at the time of arraignment. Defendants who initially were detained, either because they were denied bail and remanded or because their cash bails were high, may later gain their release through bail reviews or motions to change the original decisions. This means that comparisons of release rates and the costs of release based only on arraignment decisions will capture just part of the possible range of outcomes for defendants, and to the extent subsequent changes reduce the hurdles to pretrial freedom such comparisons may overestimate pretrial sanctioning in the jurisdictions. By the same token a focus only on the status of defendants at the time their cases are disposed of by the courts may underestimate the extent of pretrial punishment if a goodly proportion were incarcerated for varying periods of time before regaining pretrial liberty. In other words, it is necessary to determine what happens to defendants from the point they are arraigned to when their cases are concluded in order to measure fully both the scope and costs of a court's pretrial release policies. In this chapter a "pretrial punishment profile" is used so that the range of outcomes for defendants in the two cities can be determined and the extend of pretrial sanctioning adequately compared.

A second consideration in looking at policy outcomes is the part played by bondsmen in the release process. Allusions to bondsmen have been made at various points in the preceding chapters, particularly regarding the apparent collapse of Detroit's surety market that helped aggravate the situation facing Recorder's Court as it struggled to cope with its growing felony docket and overcrowding in the jail. One of the uncertainties affecting bail policies noted in Chapter 2 was the contingent nature of surety bails. Officials cannot be absolutely sure whether or when defendants will be able to post bonds, even if they can afford the premium, because the final decision rests with bondsmen. This raises a second question that must be addressed: What factors affect the performance of surety markets?

The lion's share of this chapter will be devoted to this second question, not merely because the probability of detention before trial depends on the behavior of bondsmen, and, hence, in varying degrees the severity of pretrial sanctioning, but because the efficiency of the two surety markets differed which in the end produced a policy anomaly uncovered by the pretrial punishment profiles. This discussion will help in understanding the role Detroit's surety market played in the evolution of events leading to the change in bail policies in that city. It will suggest, moreover, that two of the contextual factors used in analyzing court decision processes also assist in explaining the differential rates of surety release in the cities, namely, the risk bondsmen faced in taking felony defendants as customers in the two cities and their resources or capabilities to do so.

PROFILES OF PRETRIAL PUNISHMENT IN DETROIT AND BALTIMORE

The pretrial punishment profiles summarizing the outcomes and status of the sampled defendants and the direct costs, if any, borne by them rest on the bail histories of the defendants. These histories were traced over the course of the disposition process to ascertain the timing and content of decisions that affected the nature of the outcomes experienced by defendants. These histories were then condensed into five categories of outcomes to construct the profiles. As the accompanying table makes apparent, the categories do not describe completely the sequence and variety of changes that can occur after bail is set at arraignment; instead the profile simply depicts the major outcomes following a decision or set of decisions.

TABLE 5.1   Pretrial Punishment Profile

| | Outcome Costs Borne by Defendant | | |
Outcome Category	Posted Cash Bail	Detained in Jail	Punishment Ranking
Released on recognizance at arraignment	No	No	1 (lowest)
Released on cash bail at arraignment	Yes	No	2
Not released at arraignment; released on ROR at later stage	No	Yes	3
Not released at arraignment; released later on cash bail	Yes	Yes	4
Not released at arraignment; incarcerated until disposition	No	Yes	5 (highest)

The first two categories indicate the consequences of initial bail setting decisions. The other three reflect the fact that these early decisions may go unchanged, or be revised once or many times. The third category shows most directly the effects of bail changes since it includes only defendants previously detained on cash bails or remands who are subsequently released on their own recognizance after a bail review or pretrial motion. Defendants falling into the fourth category also ultimately gain their release, but this group includes those whose bails went unchanged in addition to those whose bails were revised. In the fifth and final category are defendants who regardless of whether or not their initial bails were revised remained in custody until the court disposed of their cases.

Based on whether defendants posted cash bails, were detained, or both, the five outcomes are ranked in the order of their presumed severity. The least punitive category includes only defendants freed on recognizance at the time of arraignment since they neither paid for their release nor were jailed. The deprivations arising from incarceration for the entire predisposition period are assumed to be more punishing than either monetary losses through cash bails alone or a combination of these losses plus some time spent in jail before the defendants regain their prearrest liberty. Accordingly, the fifth category represents the other end of the punishment spectrum. Between these two extremes three intermediate levels of pretrial punishment are identified.

Because Recorder's Court at the time of arraignment employed recognizance release more often and the bail amounts it required were lower when compared to Baltimore, it would be expected that a substantial share of the defendant sample in Detroit would have outcomes corresponding to the least punitive profile categories. Table 5.2 confirms these expectations, but only in part.

TABLE 5.2   Pretrial Punishment Profiles for Detroit and Baltimore

Outcome Category	Percent of Defendants[a]			
	Detroit		Baltimore	
Released on recognizance at arraignment	47.8		12.7	
Released on cash bail at arraignment	5.0	} 52.8	10.5	} 23.2
Not released at arraignment; released on ROR at later stage	4.1		6.8	
Not released at arraignment; released later on cash bail	11.4	} 15.5	29.4	} 36.2
Not released at arraignment; incarcerated until disposition	31.7		40.6	
Total	100.0		100.0	
Number	1,526		1,540	

[a] Only sample defendants with final disposition included.

Nearly 53 percent of Detroit's defendants avoided any period of incarceration after their arraignment. Most of them, furthermore, did not have to purchase their pretrial freedom; only 10 percent of the combined total of the first two categories were forced to post surety bail. On the other hand, Baltimore's more stringent practices restricted the likelihood of pretrial liberty at this stage. Less than a quarter, about 23 percent, of the defendants arraigned in District Court obtained their liberty without first being jailed, a difference of nearly 30 percentage points compared with Detroit. Moreover, among those who were released at arraignment, 45 percent had to make cash bail. The disparity in detention rates was narrower for the group of defendants who spent the entire predisposition period in jail, however. While still higher in Baltimore, where about 41 percent of the defendants remained behind bars compared to nearly 32 percent in Detroit, the gap had closed to roughly 9 percentage points.

In terms of either partial or full detention and the need to post money bail to secure release from custody, when contrasted to Baltimore, defendants in Detroit suffered less punitive outcomes. This is not surprising. What should attract attention, though, especially when it is recalled that cash bails were much lower in Detroit than in Baltimore, is that Detroit's proportions of defendants in the second and fourth profile categories fall short of what might be expected. Certainly they are considerably lower than those for Baltimore. Both at the time of arraignment and afterward the proportion of Baltimore's defendants freed on surety bonds was two to nearly three times greater than the proportion in Detroit, despite the fact that the latter's median bail amount was less than half that of Baltimore's. This apparent anomaly will be looked into more thoroughly after the costs of the various outcomes are presented.

Defendants not released on their own recognizance at arraignment accounted for over 85 percent of the sampled defendants in Baltimore and slightly more than half of the Detroit sample. For these defendants there were important cost dimensions to the outcomes they experienced. Surety bonds entail permanent monetary losses that can be measured by the bail premiums paid to bondsmen. The economic, social, and personal costs of incarceration are not so easily or simply determined; a crude measure, used here, is the number of days spent in jail before defendants gained their release or the court disposed of their cases. Table 5.3 indicates these two major costs for those defendants whose cases were concluded by June 13, 1973. Since defendants released on their own recognizance at arraignment suffered neither of these costs, this first profile category has been excluded from the table.

For each of the four relevant profile categories, defendants in Baltimore experienced either higher monetary costs, longer periods of detention, or both. For example, defendants who posted cash bails at their arraignment paid a median bail premium of $140, two and one-half times higher than the comparable median of $55 in Detroit. In the instance of defendants who made bail after being detained, the median bail price in Baltimore ($200) was nearly double that paid by defendants in Detroit ($110). Turning to the length of time defendants spent in jail, defendants jailed in Baltimore had longer detention periods. For those incarcerated for the entire predisposition period the contrast with Detroit was particularly striking. From arraignment to final disposition the median detention time was 141 days while in Detroit it was a mere 27 days. Moreover, with

TABLE 5.3 Mean and Median Costs of Pretrial Punishment in Detroit and Baltimore

| Outcome Category | Detroit | | | | Baltimore | | | |
| | Bail (Dollars) | | Jail (Days) | | Bail (Dollars) | | Jail (Days) | |
	Mean	Median	Mean	Median	Mean	Median	Mean	Median
Released on cash bail at arraignment	$100	$ 55 (N=76)	—	—	$195	$140 (N=154)	—	—
Not released on arraignment; released on ROR at later stage	—	—	23	7 (N=61)	—	—	33	15 (N=108)
Not released at arraignment; released later on cash bail	$223	$110 (N=168)	12	6	$252	$200 (N=447)	21	6
Not released at arraignment; detained until disposition	—	—	82	27 (N=488)	—	—	147	141 (N=631)

Baltimore's median and mean being nearly the same, this means that most of these defendants languished in the city jail for at least four months before their cases were concluded.

These detention periods for the most part depended on the case scheduling policies and speed with which the courts disposed of their caseloads. The sustained efforts made by Recorder's Court to quicken the tempo of its dispositions were described earlier. The results of these efforts show up in the fact that incarcerated defendants spent far less time in jail than defendants in Baltimore where the process was much slower. The detention periods for defendants freed on recognizance after failing to make bail or who were first remanded also reflected their policies since the median period of 7 days in Detroit and 15 days in Baltimore closely paralleled when preliminary hearings were scheduled. In Detroit they were set within a week to 10 days after arraignment; in Baltimore it was at least two weeks.

When reviewing the financial costs of the outcomes in Table 5.3, it should be kept in mind that the figures have a somewhat ambiguous meaning. The lower costs incurred by Detroit's defendants are not "better" simply because they paid in the aggregate lower prices for their freedom. From one perspective they may be since bail amounts were lower to begin with and defendants naturally incurred lesser financial losses. But this conclusion hinges on the performance of the city's surety bondsmen and whether they operated in a way that cleared the market of the demand for their services. If the market performed inefficiently for any reason or functioned cautiously by rejecting defendants with higher bails even if they were capable of paying the bondsmen's premiums, the median costs of release shown in Table 5.3 would be correspondingly lower than if all defendants with the financial wherewithal to make bail were freed by the bondsmen. In other words, the meaning or value attached to lower financial costs of pretrial freedom and whether they are preferable or not depends on the rate of release, which in cities like Detroit and Baltimore in 1972 reflects the operating efficiency of the local surety markets. It is clearly time, then, to return to the anomaly mentioned earlier since it provides the backdrop for the discussion on the political economy of surety markets that follows.

Detroit's bails were considerably lower, but its defendants with surety bonds had higher detention rates than in Baltimore. This situation is shown clearly by looking at those sampled defendants with money bails and the proportions who were released or incarcerated. Table 5.4 indicates that 64.2 percent of these defendants in Detroit failed to post bail before the disposition of their cases; in Baltimore the proportion was 45.4 percent.

When Detroit's defendants did not receive personal bonds or recognizance either at their arraignments or at other stages in the disposition process, their chances of being jailed were considerably greater than for simi-

TABLE 5.4 Outcomes for Defendants with Cash Bails in Detroit and Baltimore

Outcome Category	Percent of Defendants	
	Detroit	Baltimore
Released on cash bail at arraignment	10.9	14.4
Not released at arraignment; released later on cash bail	24.9	40.2
Not released; detained until disposition	64.2	45.4
Total	100.0	100.0
Number	698	1,127

larly situated defendants in Baltimore. This anomaly in which a city where cash bails were lower and relatively infrequent detained proportionately more defendants than a city where higher cash bails were required for most defendants warrants further exploration. The following discussion, nevertheless, should not obscure the finding presented here that outcomes in Detroit were generally far less punitive than those incurred by Baltimore's defendants.

THE POLITICAL ECONOMY OF SURETY BOND MARKETS

Why did defendants with surety bonds gain their release from custody less often in Detroit than in Baltimore? The answer to this puzzle can be found by looking at the political economies of the cities' surety markets and particularly at how the policies of the courts shaped these markets. The first factor to be considered relates to the demand for the services of bondsmen, both in the aggregate and in terms of "effective demand." The second factor pertains to the "supply" of these services which is influenced greatly by the size of surety markets, the structure of the local bonding industry, and the financial risks bondsmen take if they fail to have their clients in court for their hearings or trials.

Courts determine the size of surety markets, and hence the aggregate demand for bondsmen, according to how often they require surety bonds as a condition for pretrial freedom. For defendants who must post these bonds, however, the odds of being released are largely a function of their financial resources, or those of family members and friends, relative to the size of the bonds. Defendants obviously can purchase their liberty only when surety amounts set by courts fall within their financial means. The effective demand for bondsmen, then, reflects the size of the market and the relationship between bail amounts and defendant resources. But, when considering the relationship between surety bail amounts and the chances of release for defendants, the key variable is the size of the surety *premium*.[1]

The importance of looking at premiums rather than total bails quickly becomes evident in the case of Baltimore and Detroit. Baltimore's high bail amounts, it turns out, posed lower obstacles to the pretrial liberty of defendants than its amounts otherwise would suggest simply because of state insurance rules. Premium rates set by Maryland were 7 percent of the first $3,000 and 6 percent of any amount over $3,000. In contrast, Detroit's bondsmen charged 11 percent of the bond amount. These probably were minimum rates in both cities because bondsmen were known to charge higher premiums on occasion.[2] Indeed, according to Michigan insurance rules, Detroit's bondsmen were supposed to charge only 10 percent, but alleging that their costs of doing business had increased they had arbitrarily upped their rates.

These different rates dramatically narrowed the costs of release for defendants in the cities and in effect raised the level of effective demand in Baltimore while reducing it in Detroit. For example, a $5,000 surety bond carried a minimum premium of only $330 in Baltimore but in Detroit the same bail cost $550. With Maryland's rate structure, the total bail would have to reach approximately $8,500 before the premium would equal that paid for a $5,000 bond in Detroit. As a result, even though its bail amounts were larger, the release prices confronting Baltimore's defendants more nearly resembled those in Detroit where total bail amounts were lower but premiums were higher. Table 5.5 displays the release costs for defendants at the time of their dispositions after allowing for any revisions or changes in initial bail-setting decisions.

TABLE 5.5   Final Release Costs for Defendants with Surety Bonds in Detroit and Baltimore

Final Surety Release Costs	Proportions of Defendants	
	Detroit	Baltimore
Under $100	26.6	15.8
$100–$199	23.5	22.5
$200–$299	9.8	15.6
$300–$399	2.8	17.8
$400–$999	17.0	20.9
$1,000–$1,999	16.7	3.1
Over $2,000	3.5	4.3
Total	100.0	100.0
Number	706	1,069

While the proportion of defendants with surety premiums under $100 was higher in Detroit, when the three lower premium categories are combined, the proportions for both cities were strikingly similar. Nearly 54 percent of Baltimore's defendants had premiums under $300 compared to about 60 percent for Detroit. Also reflecting the higher premium rate levied by Detroit's bondsmen, the proportion of defendants with release costs exceeding $1,000 was nearly three times greater than that of Baltimore. Surety premium rates then are important factors behind release opportunities for defendants. Despite Detroit's lower bail amounts, defendants in this city may have been unable to purchase their release at rates that would seem consistent with its overall lower bail amounts. The

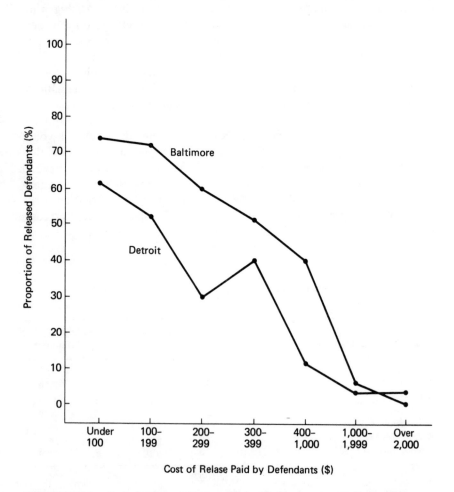

FIGURE 5.1 Proportion of Defendants Released on Surety Bonds by Cost of Release.

difference in premium rates charged by bondsmen in the cities thus provides a partial explanation for why Baltimore's defendants, in the aggregate, succeeded in purchasing their pretrial liberty more often than defendants with sureties in Detroit. But, as Figure 5.1 indicates, even when comparing defendants with similar premiums, the probability of release still remained higher in Baltimore. Could this difference be because defendants in Baltimore were better able to afford their bondman's premium than their counterparts in Detroit?

Before they can purchase their release from custody, defendants must have access to or possess the financial wherewithal to meet the bondsmen's prices. The gap in release rates revealed by Figure 5.1, therefore, may be due to differences in employment levels for the two groups of defendants. In fact, only approximately 26 percent of Detroit's felony defendants who had surety bonds to post were employed compared to 45 percent in Baltimore and, as Table 5.6 shows, at each of the various release prices Baltimore's defendants were more likely to be working than defendants in Detroit. When taken in conjunction with its lesser release prices for similar bail amounts, Baltimore's defendants apparently were better able to afford the bondsmen's fee for their freedom than defendants in Detroit.

TABLE 5.6   Proportion of Employed Defendants by Cost of Release in Detroit and Baltimore

Final Surety Release Cost	Proportion of Employed Defendants (Number)	
	Detroit	Baltimore
Under $100	28.2 (156)	41.3 (104)
$100–$199	24.5 (139)	58.0 (143)
$200–$299	23.3 (60)	31.9 (94)
$300–$399	52.6 (19)	55.2 (105)
$400–$999	25.9 (85)	38.7 (137)
$1,000–$1,999	21.8 (78)	42.4 (28)
Over $2,000	0 (10)	30.8 (26)
Average	25.8 (547)	45.1 (637)

Although employment status is a crude measure of purchasing power, data on the income or wealth of defendants, which would have been better indicators of their resources, were not available. According to the 1970 Census, however, incomes were generally lower in Baltimore than in Detroit during 1969. In both samples over 80 percent of the defendants were black, and almost all of the blacks were males. For black males 16 years old and over, the median annual income was $5,742 in Baltimore and $7,548 in Detroit. The median income for black families in Baltimore was $7,414 and in Detroit it was $8,643. Still, granting the assumption for the moment that the economic resources of defendants in the two cities were roughly the same (which gives the benefit of the doubt about income levels to Detroit), the rates of release from custody would be expected to be about the same at different premium levels. That is, the chances of employed or unemployed defendants with equivalent bail prices in the cities gaining their release would be approximately similar if monetary resources were the sole factor affecting whether they were freed or not. Figures 5.2 and 5.3 show, however, Baltimore's defendants still continued to buy their liberty at generally higher rates than defendants in Detroit regardless of employment status or bail costs.

The irregular pattern for Detroit's employed defendants probably reflects the small number of defendants in the cost categories of Figure 5.2.

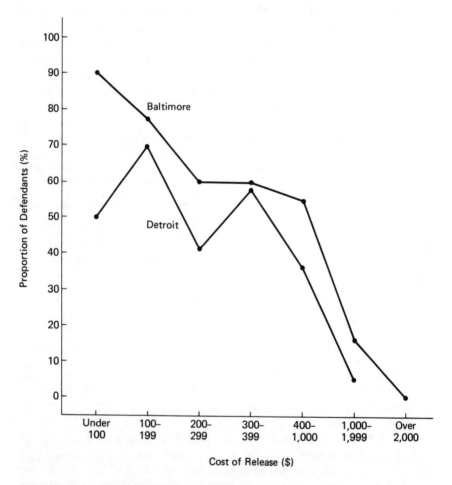

FIGURE 5.2 Proportion of Employed Defendants Released on Surety Bond by Cost of Release.

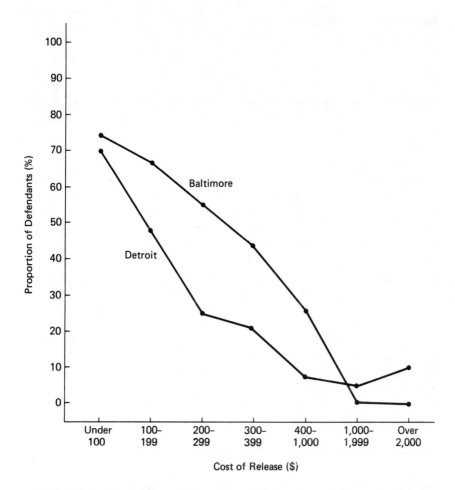

FIGURE 5.3   Proportion of Unemployed Defendants Released on Surety Bond by Cost of Release.

Such is not the case with the unemployed defendants in Figure 5.3 where each price category has ample numbers of defendants. Baltimore's persistently higher release rates, even after taking into account employment status, could have been due to the greater financial resources of its defendants, although the census data just presented indicated incomes were generally lower in Baltimore than in Detroit. There is yet another factor to be considered, however. The ability or willingness of bondsmen to write bonds for felony defendants with roughly similar economic statuses and bail costs may have differed between the two cities.

Whatever the ability of defendants to pay surety premiums, bondsmen must be willing to accept them as customers before they will be freed. Buyers of pretrial freedom need willing sellers of this freedom.

Accordingly, the differences in release and detention rates between the two cities only partially stem from similarities in the sizes of surety premiums and differences in the financial capabilities of defendants. Another critical factor, a combination of elements influencing the behavior of bondsmen, includes the size of the surety market, the structure of the bonding industry, and court policies regarding bail forfeitures. When taken together, these elements constitute incentives and risks affecting the actions of bondsmen in a city and hence the supply of bonding services.

Courts determine the size of surety markets by requiring defendants to post surety bonds for their release. Baltimore's surety market was large. Persons arrested for serious traffic violations, such as reckless driving or drunken driving, misdemeanor crimes, and felony offenses were all eligible for surety bonds when they were not granted recognizance releases. Without data on the number of traffic offenders and how many had to post bail, the exact size of this market cannot be measured fully. An approximation of its size can be gained, however, from the report by the State's Attorney Office on defendant volume in 1973 and from data in a study commissioned by District Court to assess the effectiveness of Rule 777' for the same year. Taking the State's Attorney Office's estimates of the number of misdemeanor and felony defendants and multiplying them by the percentages of misdemeanor and felony defendants released on surety bonds produces a combined total of about 10,200 defendants who were freed by bondsmen during 1973.[3]

Bondsmen in Detroit operated within a much more confined market. State bail laws in Michigan prohibited local courts from requiring surety bonds of defendants arrested for misdemeanor offenses or serious traffic violations and consequently eliminated large numbers of potential customers from Detroit's surety market. For example, in 1972 over 14,000 misdemeanor warrants were processed by the Misdemeanor Division of Recorder's Court. A further reduction in the market occurred when Recorder's Court increased its use of personal bonds for felony defendants in 1972. As a result, the potential demand for bondsmen, as measured by the total number of felony defendants with surety bonds, fell to 5,630 compared to 8,807 for 1971. The number of defendants released on surety bail shrank from 5,137 to 3,061 between the two years.[4] Comparing the size of the markets in the two cities according to the total number of defendants actually released in surety bonds, Detroit's market was probably a third the size of Baltimore's in 1972.

In addition to their dissimilar sizes, the two markets also differed in terms of how their local surety industry was organized. Bondsmen were more plentiful and more loosely organized in Baltimore compared to Detroit.[5] During 1972 five surety insurance companies with 31 agents operated in Baltimore. Seventeen of the bondsmen were solo agents with the rest organized into three firms. In Detroit, where there were just 13 representatives of only two insurance companies, the surety business was more highly structured. A single agency with 6 bondsmen and one partnership between 2 agents dominated the market. The other 5 bondsmen were individual entrepreneurs.[6] Concentration in Detroit's bonding industry was actually greater than the number of agents and firm suggests. According to the sample data, 3 bondsmen, 2 of whom were agents in the single firm, wrote 67 percent of the surety bonds in 1972. The remaining business was scattered among 8 different agents.[7] Unfortunately, comparable data on market shares in Baltimore were not available.

The degree to which the bonding business was concentrated and the size of surety markets in the two cities may have affected the opportunity for felony defendants to gain their release. In Baltimore, although the market shares of agents were unknown, it appeared through observation and interviews that no one firm or small set of bondsmen dominated the market. In addition, the large volume of traffic and misdemeanor bonds gave the city's bondsmen the opportunity to generate enough revenue to absorb losses that might arise from forfeitures of the generally higher surety bonds needed by felony defendants. Bondsmen referred to traffic and misdemeanor bonds as "gravy" or "cream" because their lower premiums were offset by their large volume and relatively low risk.[8]

This reservoir of gravy put Baltimore's bondsmen in the position to take felony defendants as customers despite their higher bonds. Moreover, if most of them had sufficiently large volumes of business based on gravy cases to consider felony bonds, Baltimore's defendants may have been able to go to more than just two or three bondsmen to have their bails posted. The combined factors of a more competitive bonding industry, or at least a greater number of bondsmen, and enough gravy to cover potentially large felony forfeitures may be the major reasons why felony defendants were more likely to be released on surety bonds in Baltimore than Detroit.

Data for Detroit provide support for this argument which essentially suggests that as the volume of surety business increases for individual bondsmen, their ability to accept defendants with higher bails also increases. Eleven different bondsmen wrote bonds for the sample defendants in this city. The average premium for the three most active ones was $201; an average surety bond of about $1,800. In contrast, the premiums of the remaining bondsmen averaged only $90, equivalent to an average surety bond of roughly $800. The higher average premium for the three major bondsmen reflected the fact that they wrote higher bonds than the others. While the bondsmen who captured most of Detroit's surety business posted bonds of $10,000 and $15,000, none of the sureties written by the other bondsmen exceeded $3,000.

It appears, therefore, than a bondsman's volume of business directly influences his ability to issue bonds for higher amounts.[9] However, the small number of bondsmen who were in this position reduced the competitiveness of Detroit's market and felony defendants with high surety bonds were forced to contact the three bondsmen capable of writing substantial surety bonds. In Baltimore, on the other hand, there may have been several bondsmen who because of the size of the surety market could write bonds for the high bails imposed by the court in felony cases. Accordingly, the differences in the proportions of defendants released on surety bonds before the disposition of their cases may have been due to the presence of more bondsmen with sufficient financial resources to accept felony defendants as customers in Baltimore compared to Detroit.

In summary, this explanation for the anomaly that defendants with cash bails in Detroit were more likely to be detained for the entire predisposition period than comparable defendants in Baltimore rests on a complex combination of three major factors. First, after converting surety amounts into premium payments defendants would have to raise for their release, the size and distribution of release prices in the cities were more similar than a consideration of the full amounts alone would have suggested. If premium rates in Baltimore had been the same as Detroit's, its rate of detention undoubtedly would have been higher. Second, Baltimore's defendants were employed more often than defendants in Detroit which allowed them to make their bails more easily. However, even unemployed defendants in Baltimore gained their release proportionately more often than Detroit's defendants. Finally, the larger surety market and greater numbers of active bondsmen in Baltimore appear to have created conditions whereby felony defendants with surety bails were able to contact several bondsmen who, with surety businesses large enough to cushion the greater losses that might arise from the forfeiture of a felony bond, were willing to gamble on these defendants.

This argument raises an interesting policy paradox for bail reformers since it states that the smaller a city's surety market, the higher the proportion of defendants who will be unable to buy their pretrial liberty and thus be detained. Thomas found much the same thing in his survey of bail practices in 20 cities for 1971. His data indicate "the increased use of nonfinancial releases has cut into the number of defendants who would have posted bail" and with few exceptions the percentage of defendants released on cash bails decreases as the use of recognizance rises.[10] Thus, the more "reformed" the pretrial policies of courts, the greater the likelihood that those defendants not released on recognizance will be detained. Courts, then, shape the financial incentives of bondsmen, and accordingly their decisions as to whom to accept as customers, but it is equally as important to consider how courts determine the costs associated with the risks facing bondsmen.

When their clients fail to appear in court, bondsmen must pay the court the full amount of the bond. The threat of this loss is their incentive to assure the defendant's court appearance. Before a bond is forfeited, bondsmen generally are given time by courts to find the defendant and bring him back into custody. If they fail in this effort and cannot locate the defendant within this period, the bond is then forfeited. Forfeiture rules as with other court rules generally vary from court to court, and Detroit and Baltimore were no exception. Recorder's Court allowed only 10 days from the time the capias or arrest warrant was issued while Baltimore permitted its bondsmen 90 days with the possibility of 60-day extensions. With less time to find a defendant before incurring the financial loss of the bond, the probability of this loss was higher for Detroit's bondsmen than for their counterparts in Baltimore.

Still, bail forfeitures, it is well to remember, do not lead invariably to permanent losses for bondsmen. Even though the time before a forfeiture may be exhausted, if a bondsman ultimately retrieves his client, the court as a matter of judicial discretion can refund the amount of the bond. In Detroit, however, a prominent bondsman reported several judges routinely deducted the amount of the premiums from bonds before refunding them. The rationale for this policy was that the court should be recompensed for the cost of being prepared for trial or for a hearing which was not held because the defendant was not there. From the bondsman's perspective, this meant that a "free" service had been rendered the court since it chose to ignore whatever time or resources were expended by the bondsman in locating the defendant. It was this policy that prompted Detroit's bondsmen to feel they were justified in charging higher premium rates than state insurance rules allowed. Interviews with Baltimore's bondsmen did not uncover comparable practices by this city's judges.

Court policies, therefore, affect both sides of the bondsman's ledger. Through their bail decisions, courts create the demand for his services and, hence, his revenues. Depending on the forfeiture policies, courts also can vary the cost associated with the risk that defendants may not appear on their court dates. If potential revenues decline because the court has increased its use of recognizance release, while the costs of forfeitures remain the same or increase, the bondsmen in a city can be expected to exercise more caution and take only those customers they feel are safe bets and whose bails they can afford to cover. This behavior may be encouraged further if the court removes the "cream" from the market. Accordingly, whether intended or not, the court will have created a set of conditions under which defendants with cash bails are less likely to gain their release compared to cities where the surety market is larger, revenues for the individual bondsmen are higher, and the forfeiture rules of the court are lax enough not to increase the costs of error for the bondsmen. The first set of conditions existed in Detroit, while the second set generally described Baltimore.

CONCLUSIONS

Persons accused of felony crimes in Baltimore were much more likely to be detained after their bail hearings than in Detroit. This rate of initial detention sprang from the strong reluctance of District Court commissioners to grant felony defendants recognizance release and, while they probably had discounted the bail amounts characteristic of the previous bail tariff, these reductions were not large enough to prevent most defendants from being jailed. In addition, Baltimore's defendants also stayed in jail longer before they regained their liberty and, of course, they paid higher prices for their freedom. For a substantial proportion of Baltimore's defendants, however, the major outcome was not freedom at a price, but long terms of pretrial detention in the Baltimore City Jail. Outcomes were less harsh in Detroit. A majority of the defendants were released after their arraignments with little or no financial costs. Surprisingly, even though Detroit's bail amounts on the whole were not as large as those in Baltimore, defendants with cash bails were no more likely than those in Baltimore to gain their release, indeed their chances were worse. Consequently, after the arraignment stage the differences between the two pretrial punishment profiles narrowed.

The finding that Baltimore's defendants with surety bonds were more, not less, likely to gain their release than Detroit defendants with surety bonds, even after taking into account premium amounts and defendants' employment status, leads to an important conclusion. Maryland's insurance rules reduced the potentially adverse effects of high cash bails in Baltimore through a rate structure that resulted in bail premiums that probably were more in line with the resources of defendants. Baltimore's larger and more lucrative surety market also allowed bondsmen to take defendants as customers whom Detroit's bondsmen would have refused or been reluctant to accept. As a final factor, the more relaxed forfeiture practices of Baltimore's courts did not penalize bondsmen to the same extent as Detroit's courts.

On the basis of this explanation, it would appear that if surety bonds are not to function as a means of either deliberate or inadvertent preventive detention, then criminal courts should pursue policies which expand the incentives of bondsmen to accept defendants with surety bonds while eliminating court-imposed costs when there are forfeitures. In thriving surety markets where bondsmen face little or no risk, defendants will be better able to avoid incarceration—to the extent that they can pay the price for pretrial freedom.

What this conclusion suggests is that more thought should be given the problem of how to create surety markets that are maximally efficient in fostering the release of defendants. Such an effort would be anathema to bail reformers and others since bondsmen are probably the most disparaged figures in American criminal courts. Yet Thomas' findings and the arguments presented here suggest that attempts to increase the use of recognizance release without consideration of their effects on the operation of surety markets may result in the emergence of a de facto policy of preventive detention which ironically may be nurtured unwittingly by the well-intended efforts of the reformers themselves.

REFERENCES

1. Observations and interviews with bondsmen in both cities indicate bondsmen did not always require collateral, although Detroit's bondsmen appeared to demand it more often than in Baltimore. This is consistent with the argument presented later on because to some extent this difference may have been due to the greater risks the bondsmen faced in Detroit in terms of the costs associated with forfeitures compared to Baltimore. See Forrest Dill, "Discretion, Exchange and Social Control: Bail Bondsmen in Criminal Court," *Law and Society Review* 9 (1975): 661–663, for evidence on this question in two other courts. In passing, it might be noted that Dill's article regrettably stands alone in its sophistication and effort at understanding the behavior of bondsmen despite the fact that they often are singled out as pivotal figures in the operation of pretrial release systems. Also, see Paul Wice, "Purveyors of Freedom: The Professional Bondsmen," *Society* 11 (1974): 34–41; and Richard L. Ramey, "The Bail Bond Practice from the Perspective of Bondsmen," *Creighton Law Review* 8 (1975): 865–892.
2. Overcharging by bondsmen became an open issue in both cities. See the *Detroit Free Press* (November 13, 1974); and Baltimore *Evening Sun* (August 26, 1970).
3. According to the State's Attorney Office, there were 31,742 misdemeanor and 5,136 felony defendants in 1973. The surety release rate was .276 for misdemeanants and .286 for felony defendants according to the report done by the National Council on Crime and Delinquency, *Pretrial Release in Maryland* (1974), see Table 8.
4. Recorder's Court, *Annual Reports* (Detroit, Mich., 1971 and 1972).
5. Information on the number of surety companies and agents in the cities was gathered from annual lists of licensed and approved bondsmen on file in the clerk offices of the courts.
6. Differences in the volume of business for the largest bondsmen were striking. According to one bondsman, who with his brother operated Detroit's major bonding firm, the firm's annual gross volume was about $4 million in 1972. For the same year in Baltimore, the gross revenue was $1 to $1.5 million for one of the city's larger surety bondsmen.
7. Two other bondsmen were licensed but did not write any surety bonds for the sample defendants.
8. The risk for bondsmen, it should be noted, does not stem from the defendant's failure to appear as much as from the size of the financial loss and whether the court demands forfeiture of the bond. This point is discussed in more detail shortly.

9. For a similar argument explaining the behavior of bondsmen in New Haven, see Malcolm M. Feeley, *The Process is the Punishment*, New York, Basic Books, 1979.

10. Wayne H. Thomas, Jr., *Bail Reform in America*, Berkeley, University of California Press, 1976, p. 43.

6

Conclusions

INTRODUCTION

Punishment before trial occurs as a result of public policies and private decisions shaped by these policies. It involves the loss of liberty, time spent in jail, and financial penalties for citizens accused but not convicted of commiting crimes. This book has sought to explain why punishment before trial differs in magnitude and severity in criminal courts and to determine the conditions under which policies affecting it are likely to change. Case studies of pretrial release practices and surety markets in two cities, Detroit and Baltimore, provided the empirical foundations for investigating these questions.

At issue is the fact that society's concern over crime and its safety often conflict with the rights of criminal defendants. This conflict is starkest in the instance of felony crimes, for society's fear of crime centers on such felonious offenses as burglary, robbery, armed assaults, or rape. Against these fears are posed the defendants' constitutional guarantees of due process and the presumption of innocence undergirding them. Criminal courts in making decisions that establish the conditions for the pretrial release of felony defendants ultimately define a balance between these conflicting expectations.

How this balance is struck and the dynamics of change when it is upset were analyzed on the basis of a conceptual framework that highlighted the political environments of courts and the influence of uncertainty, risk, and resources in creating contexts of choice. Within these contexts three modes of choice were identified that reflected more specific factors such as information, access of officials, and docket characteristics. Models of policy change and search also were developed employing this framework, and courts were presumed to use a "minimize risk" decision rule when selecting or looking for solutions to problems. Finally, in a more abbreviated manner this framework was utilized to construct a "political economy" perspective of the operation of surety bond markets and bondsman behavior.

In this concluding chapter, a brief summary of how this analytical approach helped explain the differences in the scope and cost of pretrial punishment of felony defendants in Detroit and Baltimore will be presented. After this is done, the question of policy stability will be explored further in order to provide a fuller understanding of when and how policy changes are likely to take place in criminal courts. Finally, the implications of this study for traditional bail reform efforts will be discussed.

WHY PUNISHMENT BEFORE TRIAL DIFFERS: A REVIEW OF DETROIT AND BALTIMORE

Detroit and Baltimore to a degree approximated the extremes in pretrial sanctioning of felony defendants that prevailed among larger American cities in the early seventies. In 1972 nearly 48 percent of the felony defendants arraigned in Detroit's Recorder's Court were freed on their own recognizance and the median bail amount was $2,000. The proportion of defendants detained for the entire predisposition period was about 32 percent. In Baltimore's District Court felony defendants were less likely to be released on recognizance. About 12 percent of them were released from custody on this basis at arraignment. Bail amounts were also higher compared to Detroit; the median bail was $4,650. Its detention rate was nearly 41 percent.

The political environment of Recorder's Court in 1972 was characterized by relatively strong prodefendant sentiment. This reflected a growth in disaffection with Detroit's criminal justice system and its court after the 1967 riot during which several thousand people most of whom were black were detained through exorbitant bails. As various groups formed around this issue, court policies increasingly were scrutinized according to whether they protected the rights of the accused and afforded equal justice. The decisive event, however, was the conclusion of a jail case brought by politically liberal and radical attorneys that led to the imposition of a population limit on the Wayne County Jail which had been overcrowded with primarily felony defendants awaiting court hearings or trials in Recorder's Court.

Prior to this decision, Recorder's Court had grappled with the problem of overcrowding in the jail by taking various steps to speed up the pace of its dispositions. In doing so, it had been able to avoid changing its bail policies. But by the time the Wayne County Circuit Court issued its decree, this policy alternative was no longer open to Recorder's Court. The median number of days between arraignment and disposition was only 71 days in 1972. Accordingly, the court contracted the scope of its bail policies by expanding its use of recognizance release.

One effect of this reduction in detention resources was its constraining influence on the uncertainty and risk surrounding the release of felony defendants. While judges frequently "trusted the system" when in doubt about defendants and on occasion were "jolted" by subsequent criminal behavior of defendants they did not expect would be released, and although criminal justice policies were volatile matters in Detroit's politics, the need to do something about the jail assumed paramount importance. A second consequence was that it contributed to the routine processing of bail hearings. To reduce the jail population, defendants with minor felonies, who made up a relatively large proportion of the bail docket, were granted recognizance and their cases were quickly concluded. In addition to this the judges had other work assignments, the time allotted the long bail dockets was short, and the judges felt the arraignment officer provided them with enough information that they could expedite the hearings as swiftly as possible. Compared to the routine mode of choice, the situational and bargaining modes were relatively infrequent.

In contrast to Detroit's judges, who held relatively secure positions once they reached the bench, bails were set in Baltimore by low status court officials or commissioners with insecure tenure who were more highly vulnerable to negative sanctions. The commissioners owed their positions to a larger reform of Baltimore's lower court which had been besmirched by a traffic ticket scandal. As part of this overhauling a new bail rule modeled after the 1966 Federal Bail Reform Act was drafted. Although Baltimore's Supreme Bench had created a Pre-Trial Release Division earlier to recommend and supervise defendants for recognizance release, Rule 777 and the commissioners received an unenthusiastic welcome. No ground swell of popular support had preceded it and none followed. Compared to Detroit, prodefendant sentiment was weaker in Baltimore as the police and other public officials criticized the reform as threatening the safety of the city.

This hostile setting and the commissioner's vulnerability meant they had few positive incentives to narrow the scope of bail policies, particularly for felony defendants. They saw their task, moreover, as not only a risky venture but an uncertain one as well because of inadequate or erroneous information about defendants, and they had little knowledge, aside from their mistakes, about the outcomes of their decisions. This uncertainty fostered a situational context for making decisions since commissioners turned to defendants for information or confirmation of what little they had, as well as for clues or signs that defendants could be trusted or were responsible. A mixed and light docket also facilitated this mode while heightening the perceived gravity of felonies because of their infrequency compared to the much greater number of misdemeanor cases. Finally, the commissioners were not constrained by limited detention resources despite the political furor and legal battle involving the jail, although they were hampered by the restrictive policies of the pretrial release agency.

In comparing the two cities, then, the situations facing the court officials responsible for making initial bail decisions were quite different. Detroit's judges had to revise their bail policies in order to restore some degree of equilibrium between suddenly reduced detention resources and its limited ability to dispose of cases much faster than it already was. In Baltimore the commissioners worked out incremental solutions to the meaning of reform under Rule 777 that would reduce the risks and uncertainty of change while meeting their responsibilities for implementing the reform. In doing so they used as benchmarks the bail rules and practices of the former Municipal Court as well as the bail review decisions of District Court judges to guide their decisions about bail amounts. At the same time, commissioners accommodated police requests for recognizance releases, but shunned the security bail option when financial or money bail was imposed. The reasons in both instances rested on the problem of who would be held to account for the defendant's behavior if freed.

Table 6.1 summarizes in broad terms the contrast between Detroit and Baltimore according to the basic elements of the organizational perspective introduced in Chapter 2. As this table suggests, the scope and cost

TABLE 6.1 Bail Setting Policies in Detroit and Baltimore: Environment, Context, and Mode of Choice

	Detroit	Baltimore
Political environment		
prodefendant sentiment	Stronger	Weaker
Context of choice		
uncertainty	Lower	Higher
risk and vulnerability	Lower	Higher
detention resources	Lower	Higher
Mode of choice		
primary mode	Routine	Situational
docket	Felony, long	Mixed, short
information	Reliable, complete	Unreliable, incomplete
access to officials	Low	Low
encounter with defendant	Important, varied	Very important
Scope and cost of bail-setting policy		
scope	Narrower—higher use of recognizance	Broader—lower use of recognizance
cost	Lower average bail amounts	Higher average bail amounts

of initial bail policies in the two cities reflected differences in the combined influences of the incentives and constraints characteristic of the context and modes of choice within which the court officials made their decisions.

Initial bail setting policies are not automatically translated in their totality into outcomes for defendants. With the exception of those released at arraignment either on their own recognizance or after posting cash bails, other actors and processes come into play that in varying ways can combine to exacerbate or mitigate the potential effects of these policies. Again, the two cities differed in numerous respects.

Changes in initial bail decisions occurred more often in Baltimore than in Detroit and generally these reviews relaxed the stringency of earlier decisions. On the other hand, these changes took place after a longer period of time had elapsed because of Baltimore's case scheduling practices which meant that defendants remained in jail longer before being released on recognizance or lower cash bail. And, of course, for those who never made bail the slowness with which Baltimore's courts disposed of its felony caseload meant that these defendants spent substantial time behind bars. In contrast Detroit's more swiftly moving court lessened the costs of pretrial detention for those who failed to make bail immediately after their arraignment.

Surprisingly, a mitigating factor in Baltimore that reduced the probability of pretrial detention for felony defendants was the efficiency of its surety market. Maryland's insurance rules reduced the prices of pretrial liberty to levels closer to those in Detroit even though total bail amounts were higher. Moreover, "gravy" generated through a large volume of misdemeanor surety bonds, a low risk regulatory environment, and competitive industry structure resulted in bondsmen accepting felony defendants as customers at proportionately higher rates than Detroit's bondsmen. Bondsmen in this latter city operated in a low demand, higher risk environment, were less competitively organized, and were more selective in choosing their customers by requiring collateral in addition to the bond premium.

The pretrial punishment profiles that measured the outcomes of initial bail policies and captured the effects of intervening factors on these outcomes were based on the bail histories of the sampled felony defendants. Both the profiles and the costs of various outcomes indicated that more defendants incurred higher levels of pretrial punishment in Baltimore than in Detroit. Punishment before trial, therefore, differed in the two cities for reasons that were related to the political environment and the context and modes of choice affecting initial bail decisions as well as for reasons that were related to the operation of the criminal disposition process and local surety market. A systematic explanation of why these differences occurred was a major goal of this study. A second purpose was to identify the conditions and processes of policy change. The following section takes up this concern in more detail by focusing on the stability of these policies.

SLACK RESOURCES AND POLICY STABILITY

The dynamics of policy change have been a major concern of this study. At the conclusion of the Detroit case study, a political choice model depicting the conditions and sequence of actions criminal courts take in response to a jail crisis centering an overcrowding was presented. This model was modified after reviewing events in Baltimore to incorporate whether jail problems are translated into overcrowding issues and whether bail policies are controversial. It was then simplified into a more general policy search model to indicate when and where solutions would be sought to problems arising from the jail.

The Question of Environmental Flux

These models, it should be stressed, do not rest on deterministic assumptions. It would be erroneous to think once the process is initiated that courts inevitably or quickly move through the various stages to the point where the focus is solely on revamping initial felony bail setting policies. Instead, the process is highly contingent on events and the political climate at each stage in the sequence. Progression from one point to the next and the time between stages depends on the rapidity with which incidents occur and accumulate, on the confluence of what might be normally separated events, and even on "chance events."

In Baltimore, for example, a major jail riot followed by litigation in federal court, controversy over the warden's actions leading to his dismissal, labor unrest among jail guards, and other inmate disturbances all took place within little more than two years. Without this rapid succession of events and the embarrassement they caused a recently elected mayor, it is unlikely the crisis would have reached a head. Overlaying these events, yet separate from them, was the overhauling of Baltimore's lower court, its bail rules, and the creation of a new set of officials to implement the rules. It is difficult to say with confidence whether the tarnished reputation of the previous lower court, beside the newness and controversy of the commissioner system, precluded consideration of more drastically changing arraignment bail policies to achieve the mayor's goal of reducing the jail population. The court had not yet found its political footing, in part because it suffered from its previous history. The chief judge in an interview, for instance, said he was a personal friend of the Baltimore *Sun's* publisher. But the publisher had told him that he would not approve editorial praise for the new court until certain judges implicated in the traffic ticket scandal were removed from the bench. Finally, the unexpected and unpredictable shooting deaths of police officers made the court and commissioners lightning rods of public and police anger over the release of criminal defendants. Further reform of initial bail decisions became politically even riskier than it might have been otherwise.

Viewing the dynamics of change as a highly contingent process has implications for how political environments of courts are conceptualized. It may be tempting to hastily summarize the policy differences between Detroit and Baltimore as simply being consistent with their local political cultures. Pretrial punishment in Detroit was lower for felony defendants because it is a "liberal" city, while pretrial sanctioning was higher in Baltimore because it is a "conservative" city. The problems with this effort at simplifying a complex phenomenon are twofold.

First, it ignores the fact that courts are often affected by actions taken by other courts or by state authorities that reverberate throughout the local criminal justice system and possibly cut across a city's ideological grain. The existence of these opportunities provides leverage for changing local practices. Examples of these external shocks to local courts include Rule 777 and the lawsuits filed against the jails. Secondly, local conditions underlying court policies may be more transitory than often thought with the result that ensuing policy changes may run counter to what was considered to be a "liberal" or "conservative" community. Events, groups, and a "climate of concern" may combine and recombine in different ways over time to produce uncertain and shifting environments for courts. None of this is intended to rule out of hand the existence of local norms and mores that form a generalized backdrop to criminal issues and court policies. But the notion that there is a direct and clear line between local and political culture and the extent of pretrial punishment should be held lightly.

The simplest way of illustrating what has been said here is to review quickly the situation in Baltimore after this study was completed. Despite the mayor's decree in 1973 the jail population failed to stay within the limit he had set for it. In March 1975 the population reached 1,850 prisoners, three-quarters of whom were awaiting trial. Unlike the 1971 legal challenge, lawsuits on behalf of the inmates that focused on overcrowding resulted in court orders to reduce the jail's population. No cap was imposed, however, and consequently the jail still exceeded its capacity by one-third during 1976.

Nonetheless, because of the pressure brought about by this second crisis, the Pre-Trial Release Division expanded its staff so that all defendants would be interviewed before their arraignment in District Court. To expedite the caseload, an arraignment court to screen defendants who wanted to plead guilty was created and the courts put top priority on trying jailed defendants. The scope of pretrial punishment also contracted. In 1973 the proportion of all defendants charged with misdemeanor or felony crimes released on recognizance was about 40 percent and the proportion detained until disposition was 27 percent. In 1976 the recognizance rate had jumped to 69 percent and the detention rate had dropped to 13 percent.[1] Baltimore, then, because of continuing jail problems, had moved to a relatively "liberal" overall bail policy. As will be seen shortly, the same kind of reversal occurred in Detroit.

A major difficulty in adopting a contingency perspective regarding policy change is that it fails to provide a totally satisfying answer to the nagging question: "When is change in the scope and cost of pretrial sanctioning likely to occur?" The preceding vignette, the case studies, and the models based on them point to the role of jail problems, particularly overcrowding, and perhaps "chance" in the case of Rule 777, which might not have existed without a lower court scandal and a handful of attorneys willing to exploit an opportunity for reform. There is, however, another but related approach to answering this question that deserves exploration if the groundwork for understanding criminal court policy processes is to be completed. Essentially, this approach concentrates on the stability of pretrial release policies as a function of resource slack and directs attention to the possibility that there may be limits to a court's ability to balance the conflicting demands it faces through its policies.

Policy Limits and the "No Slack Condition"

Reductions in the stringency of pretrial release policies in tandem with acceleration of case disposition procedures may not be able to continue indefinitely as palliatives to jail problems without running into political and institutional obstacles. If this is the case, it has significant implications regarding the stability of what might be called the "no slack condition" for minimal pretrial sanctioning. That is, the scope and costs of pretrial punishment are likely to be minimal when, assuming the jail functions primarily as a felony pretrial detention facility, no detention slack through overcrowding is possible and there is no slack in the disposition process. Under these conditions, the maximum number of defendants will be released on recognizance to avoid jail overcrowding consistent with its capacity; bail amounts when imposed will be low and quickly posted; and those who are detained will spend minimal periods in jail before their cases are disposed of by the courts.[2]

The instability of the no slack condition can be illustrated by looking at events in Detroit after 1972. In most respects, except for its surety market, Detroit in 1972 closely approximated this condition. Roughly half of its felony defendants were freed on their own recognizance at arraignment, bail amounts were relatively low, and for defendants who were jailed, incarceration also was relatively brief. Finally, Recorder's Court moved its docket swiftly during 1972. These policies persisted through 1973.

Policies and conditions began to shift during 1974, however.[3] The recognizance release rate at arraignment slipped to 44 percent. It fell further in 1975 to 35 percent, and by 1976 it had plummetted to 28 percent, a full 20 percentage points below what it had been four years earlier. The jail population started to rise with these changes. During the fall of 1975 it regularly soared above 900 persons. Recorder's Court judges argued that a rising number of cases involving violent crimes and the use of weapons required them to tighten their bail practices. The presiding judge felt that to have done otherwise would have sacrificed the security of Detroit's citizens. Accordingly, the court could do little about the jail's violation of its population limit. As the presiding judge told the newspapers in January of 1976, "Right now, nearly every inmate in the jail is hard-core, people who have committed several crimes, are charged with multiple crimes, or murderers who cannot be released on bond."[4]

In 1975 defendants arraigned on serious felony charges did make up a larger proportion of all arraigned defendants than in 1972. Persons accused of committing crimes against persons went from 22.1 percent in 1972 to 27.4 percent in 1975. Armed robbery and rape cases in particular rose sharply.[5] Breaking and entering or burglary defendants represented 15.4 percent of the defendants in 1975 compared to 12.4 percent in 1972.

Unlike the early seventies, mounting caseloads were not a factor behind the rise in jail population nor a problem in Recorder's Court at this time. In 1975 the volume of arraigned defendants was 12,012 and by 1976 it was 12,451; both were increases compared to 1972 when the volume was roughly 11,800 but insignificant when compared to the numbers of defendants that surged through the court in 1971. The jail population, then, had increased in part because of more stringent bail policies, but the volume of defendants played little part in the rise. What did happen as a second major factor was a striking slowdown in Recorder's Court disposition tempo.

Despite the addition of 7 new judges to the bench in 1972, bringing it from 13 to 20 judges, the court's backlog began to grow. At the conclusion of 1972, Recorder's Court reported a total of 2,051 pending or open cases. By the end of 1975 the comparable number had grown to 3,234 cases awaiting preliminary examination, pretrial conferences, or trials; and in 1976 the figure was reported to be 4,800. Behind this rising backlog was a decline in the court's productivity. The average number of cases disposed by the 13 regular judges in 1972 was 800 cases. In both 1975 and 1976 the average was about 550 cases.[6] Guilty pleas also decreased as a proportion of all concluded cases. In 1972 the proportion was 69 percent, but it fell to 53 percent in 1975 and to 54 percent in 1976. Finally, there was a dramatic lengthening in the time the court took to dispose of its cases. In 1976 it reported an overall average of 220 days from arraignment to final disposition.

With less liberal bail policies and a deterioration in Recorder's

Court's efficiency, the jail population grew and a second crisis emerged. Wayne County Circuit Court ordered the sheriff to refuse any prisoners if their admission would breach the limit it had established in 1972. In turn Recorder's Court, rather than bowing to the need to adhere to the population limit, threatened the sheriff that if he did *not* admit those defendants it felt should not be released it would hold him in contempt of court.

To avoid a showdown between the two courts, defendants were crammed into police lock-ups at the department's headquarters and in the precincts. But because none of these facilities met the standards set by the circuit court decree in 1972, several lawyers announced that they would seek a court ruling preventing the police from detaining prisoners for more than 24 hours. The crisis began to abate after the mayor opened up space in the Detroit House of Correction, a facility for convicted offenders, for 240 prisoners from the jail. Ultimately, the County Board of Commissioners placed a bond issue on the May 1976 ballot for the construction of a new jail. The voters passed the bond issue by a 3 to 1 margin. With a projected capacity of 550 prisoners, the new jail, which will operate in conjuction with the old one, will provide Recorder's Court with a major expansion in detention resources.

In Detroit, then, the policy balance struck by the court after the reduction in resources in 1972 was upset for both external and internal reasons. Recorder's Court, concerned over what it perceived as a worsening crime situation, responded by expanding the scope of pretrial punishment by limiting its use of recognizance release. At the same time, it met growing difficulties in maintaining the disposition pace it had set for itself in 1972. The problem the court quickly encountered, however, was the fact that the population cap on the jail prohibited the creation of detention slack through overcrowding. As it happened, a system-wide crisis erupted that in the end led to the temporary expansion of detention resources through the use of the Detroit House of Correction and a permanent increase in resources after the construction of the new jail.

Slack and Stability

This discussion has had two purposes. First, as with the earlier vignette about Baltimore, it is important to emphasize the point that conditions both external and internal to a court can change relatively quickly with the result that policies affecting the pretrial punishment of felony defendants change accordingly. More specifically, the Detroit case suggests that the ability and willingness of courts to revise continuously their policies in accordance with detention constraints may be limited. Like the jail, they are not infinitely elastic means of coping with problems. These limits may be defined environmentally in the case of pretrial release policies and institutionally defined in the instance of its disposition policies. A second related purpose is to suggest that the no slack condition under which punishment of felony defendants before their trials is minimized may be inherently unstable. Maximum "reform" in the sense of extensive use of recognizance, relatively low rates of detention, and minimal periods of pretrial incarceration may be relatively short-lived. To guide the following discussion, Table 6.2 portrays four combinations of slack conditions and the hypothesized stability of pretrial release policies for each combination.

TABLE 6.2   Slack Conditions and the Stability of Felony Pretrial Release Policies

Detention Slack?	Disposition Slack?	
	Yes	No
Yes	Most stable	Moderately stable
No	Moderately stable	Least stable

Policies influencing pretrial sanctioning may be least stable when there is little or no detention slack, i.e., overcrowding for whatever reason is not feasible and the jail's function cannot be changed to create additional space for felony defendants, and when there is no disposition slack, i.e., the court has approached its maximum pace given existing resources and procedures. Initial bail policies may remain undisturbed so long as crime conditions do not worsen, law enforcement activities and priorities do not shift, or there is no public hue and cry over "crime in the streets." If any of these factors does arise, the absence of detention slack means pretrial release policies cannot be tightened without leading to overcrowding since the option of quickening the disposition tempo to compensate for the influx of new jail prisoners is not feasible.

If, on the other hand, the disposition pace slackens for various reasons, the cost of pretrial incarceration will rise since detained defendants will wait longer for their trials. In the meantime, the jail's population will tend to rise, perhaps exceed its capacity, and bring with it legal or political problems for the court. A higher priority may be placed on moving cases of jailed defendants to avoid this difficulty, but may lead to other problems as the time to disposition for defendants free on bail becomes longer. The other alternative to prevent the growth in the jail population is to relax bail policies, but this may jeopardize the court's political support. Thus, to summarize what has been said, because slack affords courts with opportunities to adjust to changing conditions, its absence places the court's policies in a precarious balance that may persist only as long as the external and internal factors affecting these conditions remain relatively unchanged.

Pretrial release practices are likely to be most stable, therefore, when there is a relative abundance of both detention and disposition slack. Overcrowding provides a way of absorbing seasonal fluctuations in defendant volumes, periodic crackdowns on crime, or shifts in the severity of charges lodges against defendants without altering standard or habitual bail practices. The presence of dispositional slack, e.g., the availability of judges who can be reassigned from civil to criminal dockets, provides resources to process increases in caseloads. Accordingly, rises in the jail population can be moderated even if only normal disposition times are maintained, again without resorting to revision in bail policies. The scope and cost of pretrial punishment, it might be noted, are not necessarily greatest under this set of conditions. This would depend on those factors outlined in this study. But by the same token this "full slack" condition would not lead to its minimization.

The remaining two combinations of slack conditions are hypothesized as leading to moderate stability in pretrial sanctioning policies. In those cases where there is detention slack but no disposition slack, bail policies need not be revised to prevent jail overcrowding. For a time the inflow of pretrial detainees may exceed the outflow, but if this imbalance leading to overcrowding is relatively temporary, the jail production will decline eventually to its earlier level. In the fourth and last situation where there is disposition slack and no detention slack, efforts aimed at faster dispositions, if successful, may maintain the jail's population at its maximum level without greatly exceeding it for long stretches of time. Again, this would obviate the need to revamp bail practices at the arraignment stage. In both of these two cases, however, the question of time—how long overcrowding in the jail is tolerated, and how long the court can keep up its faster disposition pace—makes the probability of future changes in bail policies higher than if neither of these constraints existed.

As with the process models introduced earlier, this discussion shares the assumption that courts prefer to avoid the risks of relaxing their felony bail policies. Slack provides them with ways of adjusting to changing environments and shifting events, and thus buffers the court's bail policies from these effects. Accordingly, these policies are likely to be more stable than if the no slack condition prevails. By thinking about the conditions under which bail policies are likely to be stable, another dimension is added toward understanding the evolution or dynamics of policy change in criminal courts. It is possible that given similar environmental shocks courts will respond in different ways that can be explained in part by looking at the kind and amount of slack that exists.

IMPLICATIONS FOR REFORM

Reform in the traditional sense has not been a central focus of this book. Instead, criminal courts have been viewed as balancing their social control and due process responsibilities or demands within frequently turbulent environments. Policy changes, when they occurred, were treated as responses to these disturbances and not as planned efforts to change the behavior of participants in the criminal justice process to attain some predetermined goal. Less attention was paid to determining the effectiveness of the reforms that did exist in the two cities than to how they affected the context of choice in the courts as just one of several factors influencing how court officials adjusted to local political and institutional incentives. It would be remiss to ignore, however, the lessons the case studies provide regarding bail reform and the implications of this book's theoretical perspective for thinking about reform. In keeping with the concern of this study, the major focus of this concluding discussion will be on the effect of reform on minimizing the extent and cost of pretrial punishment for felony defendants.

Context versus Process

Context is more important than process in determining the scope and severity of felony pretrial punishment. This marks a reversal of the customary emphasis of bail reforms that focus on the way bail deliberations are conducted. Pretrial release agencies, cut from the pattern first drawn by the Manhattan Bail Project in the early sixties, now number more than 120, and most large cities have adopted some form of this innovation.[7] The operating premise of this reform is that by collecting and verifying information about the community ties of defendants, assessing their likelihood of appearing in court, recommending for recognizance those deemed to be safe risks, and supervising them during the pretrial period, over time the scope of punishment will contract. Essentially, then, the reform seeks to enhance the rationality of the decision process through more complete and reliable information, to orient it toward the consideration of assuring the court appearance of defendants, and to offer an alternative to surety bonds.

Admittedly, the two case studies in this book do not provide a basis for assessing the impact of this reform. In Detroit during 1972 the recognizance program did not conduct prearraignment interviews. Similarly in Baltimore, the pretrial release agency did not allocate sufficient personnel to interview every felony defendant arraigned in District Court. More importantly, the Pre-Trial Release Division's policies, it was argued in Chapter 4, hobbled the commissioners' use of the agency. Still, given the potential bias in the information gathered by the arraignment officer in Detroit's Recorder's Court and the information problems that Baltimore's commissioners suffered, it is an easy step to conclude that if these agencies had been more thoroughly involved in initial bail hearings, a greater proportion of felony defendants would be released on recognizance, other forms of nonfinancial bail, or lower bails.

This conclusion, however, may lead to confusing cause with effect. It is significant that in both cities jail crises prompted changes in agency rules or operations. Baltimore's second jail crisis resulted in an extension of its agency's operations to encompass prearraignment interviews. Detroit's program also began conducting interviews prior to arraignment and making release recommendations in 1975 when its second jail crisis began to erupt. In Baltimore the proportion of all defendants released on recognizance went up, but in Detroit the proportion went down. It is difficult to attribute all or even may of these changes as being solely due to the impact of these reforms on the character of the hearings.[8] In other words, environmental problems, i.e., jail overcrowding, concern over serious crime, and accompanying legal and political difficulties, all led to changes in the operation of the agencies and in the recognizance release rates.

The problem, however, is that these reforms can do little to alter in a fundamental way the incentives shaping the discretion of officials and how it is used when setting bails for felony defendants. Uncertainty and risk are two such incentives that in combination tend to produce levels of pretrial punishment that may be unwarranted or unnecessary. From a decion-making perspective this means that court officials may tend to overestimate the likelihood that they will release defendants on recognizance or low bail who will fail to appear in court or commit further crimes, but underestimate the chances of detaining or imposing bail costs on defendants when neither is necessary.[9]

Pretrial release agencies have little leverage over changing the political risks of freeing felony defendants. Indeed, they may be influenced by the same concerns as the court, as indicated by the use of the excluded offense rule by Baltimore's pretrial release agency. It is also worth noting that in 1979 more than half of 119 agencies surveyed in a study precluded varying proportions of defendants from being interviewed solely on the basis of their charge. Typically, as might be expected, these exclusions involved serious or violent felony crimes; about 75 percent of the agencies with this policy excluded either all felony defendants or those charged with certain specific charges.[10]

Pretrial release agencies could have some impact on the uncertainty surrounding the release of felony defendants by providing more and better information. There are two weaknesses to this solution. First, pretrial release organizations historically and currently have been reluctant to address explicitly the issue of whether a defendant poses a danger to the community or is likely to commit additional crimes if released. In felony cases, however, this often is the central question. The question by default lies in the hands of the court or is handled in a sub rosa fashion by emphasizing the likelihood of flight. The next problem, which is not unrelated to this issue, has to do with the validity of the theories underlying the selection and weighting of information regarding the future behavior of persons accused of felony crimes.

One theory focuses on the probability of future criminal behavior and essentially assumes the past is prologue. Defendants with lengthy histories of criminal involvement, and possibly emotional instability, who are accused of serious crimes are presumed as likely to continue their illegal activities. Preventive detention through high bails is frequently the result. The other two theories center on the probability of failure to appear and while to a degree of competing perspectives, they are also complementary.

The first theory might be called the "rational defendant" model. According to this perspective, the behavior of persons accused of crimes is governed by their expectation of conviction and punishment. When the charge is serious, the odds of being found guilty are high, and the probable sentence is severe, the defendant is considered to have solid motives for evading prosecution. Accordingly, stringent bail is called for. When the converse set of conditions applies, less restrictive pretrial conditions are warranted. The next perspective on the defendant's willingness to flee is the "social defendant" theory that took form with the Manhattan Bail Project and originated with research by Foote and Beeley.[11] In this model, community ties, social relationships, and personal characteristics are restraints on the defendant's behavior. When the defendant's roots in the community are deep, the risk of conviction and punishment are offset by these ties, the likelihood of flight is reduced, and less restrictive pretrial conditions are deemed necessary.

The ubiquitous finding that criminal charge and other related variables are most often strongly associated with bail decisions suggests that either the rational defendant or the bail crime model holds sway in criminal courts. This assumes, of course, that these results are not the consequences of simple habit or of using bail as retribution for committing crimes. At the same time, it bears noting that because both of these theories employ the same variables, it is difficult to tell on the basis of actual decisions and their correlates which goal and theory animated the final choice.[12]

The critical point here is that the validity of each of these theories has been questioned. Attempts to predict bail crime or violent behavior have been less than successful.[13] Nor is it clear from studies what contribution the threat of conviction and punishment makes to the motivation of defendants to elude the grasp of the courts.[14] Finally, the methods incorporating the basic dimensions of the social defendant perspective of failure to appear also have been shown to be wanting in predictive power.[15] The essential difficulty with all these "theories" is that the proportion of defendants who are rearrested or fail to show up in court is a small proportion of the released defendant population. Thus, on the basis of statistical evidence, it is possible to predict with some accuracy the successes, but not the failures, of release decisions.[16] Yet it is the failures, especially the cases of bail crime, that attract attention and become politically salient, as the Detroit and Baltimore case studies showed.

Systematic quantitative attempts to determine the validity of these theories do not hold much promise for the development of objectively based, highly accurate predictive schemes that can reduce the uncertainties of bail decisions. In fact, most pretrial release agencies do not question the applicability of the methods they have borrowed more or less intact from the Manhattan Bail Project. Only 12 percent of the agencies surveyed in 1979 that used some form of this project's "Vera Scale" for weighting information to assess the community ties of defendants tested its validity for their local conditions.[17] Ultimately, then, whether a pretrial release agency helps reduce the uncertainties of court officials regarding the release of felony defendants may depend less on the "technocratic" premise of the reform and its methods than on whether they can gain the trust of the court officials.[18] It is well to recall in this respect the finding mentioned briefly in Chapter 2 that directors of pretrial release agencies ranked maintaining good relations with judges as their primary goal. Maximizing the number of persons released prior to final disposition was ranked fourth.[19]

Based on what has been discussed here, there are two implications for thinking about this reform. First, to the extent that pretrial release agencies must gain the confidence of the courts, their effectiveness as "change agents" may be quite muted. The court's priorities tend to become the agency's priorities as suggested by the relationship between Baltimore's Supreme Bench and its pretrial release agency. Aggressive challenges to these priorities threatened this relationship, which is the basis of the organization's survival.[20] Second, the evolution of pretrial release agencies can be viewed in terms of solutions waiting for problems to occur. Unless problems crop up with some regularity, the agency may ossify. Changes in operational policies and scope of activities may come slowly or not at all until crises erupt, as suggested by the events in both Detroit and Baltimore. Indeed, depending on the extent of its institutionalization in the court system, the absence of crises may well dissipate the perceived need for the agency and undermine its chances for survival. In the case of both of these implications, a central point emerges. Pretrial release organizations as administrative resources for courts are dependent on them, and thus unlikely to effect changes in how courts use their discretion.

The key contextual factor that can constrain the effects of uncertainty and risk on the choice behavior of court officials and restrain the use of discretion is the jail; specifically, its detention capacity and whether overcrowding is either legally or politically prohibited. As the case studies and shorter vignettes in this chapter showed, the role of the jail is extremely important in determining the feasibility of pretrial sanctioning. At the same time, it is crucial to point out that the willingness or unwillingness of other courts to act on the issue of overcrowding can effect a rearrangement of the local relationships between incentives and resources that shape existing bail policies.

The lessons here are twofold. First, reducing the detention capacity of the local jail may be the most direct and quickest reform capable of minimizing the scope of pretrial sanctioning for felony defendants. This depends, however, on whether the jail functions primarily as a felony pretrial detention center. If not, other adjustments may be made that mitigate the effect of the change for felony defendants while benefitting misdemeanants who otherwise might be detained pending trial or sentenced to serve time in the jail after conviction. The second lesson is that since pretrial release policies reflect the local court's efforts at balancing the conflicting demands placed on it, given the limits of its resources, effective reform may only occur when this balance is altered by authorities not caught up in the local court's political milieu or at least willing to act despite it. The contrast between the decisions of the federal judge in Baltimore and the Wayne County Circuit Court judges in 1972, as well as the difference in court attitudes by 1975 in Baltimore, make this point clear.

Besides the pivotal consequences of reductions or limitations in detention resources, changes in court rules can make a difference in the use of discretion. Again, it is critical to note that in the instance of Baltimore this change came as a result of actions taken by authorities outside the local political system. Moreover, the opportunity for these actions arose at a critical juncture in the city's lower court history because of the traffic ticket scandal. Sufficient data to determine the net impact of Rule 777 were not available, but it does appear to have had an effect. To the extent Municipal Court bail rules were followed, recognizance releases for felony defendants probably were higher and bail amounts lower after Rule 777 went into effect and the commissioners took their posts.

What makes this case particularly interesting in considering whether bail reform is likely to have an effect is that Rule 777 was an "optional" reform.[21] It was not mandatory that the commissioners grant recognizance release to any felony defendants. Rule 777 merely stated that with the exception of capital offenses, all defendants were presumed eligible for this kind of release if commissioners judged they were likely to appear in court. Nor did the rule mandate reductions in the amounts of cash bails. It did, of course, require commissioners to consider security or deposit bail whenever financial conditions for release seemed warranted, but unlike states such as Illinois or Oregon it did not eliminate the surety bond option. With this mandatory feature absent from Rule 777, security bond was rarely used by commissioners, a pattern that persisted at least until 1976.[22]

Change, albeit relative to the history of Baltimore's lower court, did occur despite the optional quality of Rule 777. Nimmer, in one of the few efforts to develop a comprehensive view of reform and system change in courts, states as a basic proposition that "system impact occurs only if a reform supplies incentives *sufficient* to overcome existing motivation."[23] This proposition is derived from an earlier statement about the systemic sources buttressing the status quo. According to Nimmer:

> This systemic tendency to retain the status quo can . . . be understood in terms of the existence of behavioral norms within the judicial process. These informal norms are a by-product of repeated interaction among [participants].[24]

It is important from this perspective to keep in mind that along with the rule, the commissioners and their posts also were new to the lower court. Although most of them had held previous positions in either the pretrial release division or police department, they were not participants in a previous system suddenly forced to follow a new rule and to revise old habits. Thus, the reform did not have to overcome or change the motivations of officials that reflected ongoing accommodation to the interests and demands of others. In a real sense, then, the commissioners were the reform since they had to define the meaning of Rule 777. Moreover, the District Court's chief judge created expectations or norms among commissioners that they were a break from the past.[25] Optional reform under these conditions was able to produce changes, although these changes took the form of limited use of recognizance for felony defendants, satisficing solutions to the problem of excessive bail, and accommodations with the police regarding the release of certain defendants. Rule 777 and expectations regarding the role of commissioners did lead to somewhat different use of discretion, but these were not the only incentives or factors shaping the scope and cost of pretrial punishment in Baltimore.

Changes in context, in summary, can exert influence on criminal court pretrial release policies. On the basis of this study, however, these changes are most likely to occur when external actors or authorities are willing and capable of acting in ways that ignore the adjustments court officials have made to their local context and that force realignments in these adjustments. Another consideration that cannot be slighted is the importance of crises or times of intense strain that offer opportunities for change, and in most instances these crises will lead to change only if they become politicized.

In this respect, this study's conclusions differ substantially from Nimmer's view that:

> The judicial process is an essentially closed system in which the behavior of individual participants is more strongly influenced by the actions and expectations of other participants in the system than by external factors . . . . To a significant degree this closed system defines and pursues its own priorities independant of the local political system. Direct political influence occurs only sporadically.[26]

Sporadic political influences, however, may represent major inflection points in the evolution of local bail policies. Reductions in detention resources and rule changes do not eliminate discretion but they can constrain or redirect it. By the same token, it should be mentioned that the construction of new jails or their expansion, and changes in rules that mandate the automatic detention of persons accused of certain felony crimes or who are rearrested for particular crimes while on pretrial release, can deflect local policies in the opposite direction. In other words, the infrequency of such events, which emerge through the political system, may be inversely related to their importance. A second observation is that bail policies regarding felony defendants may be similar to sentencing after conviction in that they both tend to have higher public visibility than the policy areas Nimmer investigated. Since they both touch the sensitive political nerve of whether the court is protecting the public, the court may find it more difficult to close itself off from its environment.

The Place of Process

If context weighs most heavily on the choice behavior of court officials, what role does process play? Certainly, the modes of choice identified in this study would not satisfy the expectations of bail reformers. The routine mode is not conducive to the individualization of bail decisions. Moving swiftly from one case to another, bail conditions, especially bail amounts, are not likely to be tailored to the personal circumstances of defendants. The situational mode moves more leisurely and the role of the defendant is heightened. But demeanor during a bail hearing may have little to do with the behavior of the defendant if he or she is freed, yet the conditions of pretrial liberty may reflect how well or poorly the defendant performed in the eyes of court officials during the bail hearing.[27] Bail decisions made through the negotiating mode reflect the nature of the relationship between court officials and lawyers, or as in Baltimore, the accommodations officials make with police officers. In this last mode, representatives for defendants may be able to persuade court officials to establish pretrial conditions for defendants that they otherwise would not have obtained or that other similar defendants without such representation do not receive.

It is doubtful that reforms aimed at creating an adversarial mode or process will be greatly effective. While this statement clearly goes beyond the empirical basis of this book, other studies suggest that defense attorneys on whom the burden falls to assure that their clients receive the least restrictive release conditions possible face tactical problems and dilemmas. In one court, attorneys were reluctant to lose their credibility with judges or magistrates by arguing for low bails or recognizance in every case.[28] They picked and chose cases that they thought were "winners" or those they felt they could argue successfully for low bails. Even in more narrowly focused hearings involving homicide cases, another study found defense attorneys did not always seek the release of their clients if it meant that they would reveal their defense strategies, since the strength of the evidence in the cases often was a key issue in setting bail.[29]

As these comments suggest, issues of individualization and equitable treatment arise as problems in the way bail decisions are made. This study can address these problems is only a limited fashion, since its major concern has been to identify the conditions under which pretrial punishment is minimized or maximized. Perhaps the fundamental problem, however, is that bail hearings are conducted in most courts for all felony defendants, as in Detroit, and in other places such as Baltimore, for all misdemeanor defendants as well. Regardless of the particular decision mode, errors of both commission and omission may be more likely under these conditions than if the hearings dealt only with defendants presumed to be poor risks.

An excellent illustration of the errors of commission that occur when all felony defendants have bail hearings can be found in the hijacking case in Detroit. Defendants who had the misfortune of coming before the judge who had made the bail decision for the defendants who fled to Cuba found themselves with the need to post surety bonds despite the fact that their charges were varied and dissimilar to those of the absconding defendants. If they had been arraigned before the incident, they probably would have been released on their own recognizance. The chief judge of Baltimore's District Court also alluded to a similar reaction among the commissioners after the shooting deaths of the police officers. Finally, a Detroit judge talked about the difficulties he had in trying to prevent "jolts" from influencing his decisions. Errors of omission may occur for numerous reasons in all of the decision modes, as suggested earlier. Defendants who could be released safely on minimal bail or recognizance may go unnoticed in the rush of the routine mode, while attorneys may make mistakes in identifying defendants whom the judge might be persuaded to release on minimal bonds or recognizance.

The place of process in pretrial release policies, therefore, may be too broadly defined currently. Concern with the procedural aspects of due process by conducting a bail hearing for every felony defendant well may conflict in actual practice with its substantive aspects. If bail hearings were held only for those felony defendants who were deemed most likely to flee the jurisdiction or who were considered to be a serious danger to the community, the "spillover" effect of mistakes and jolts and perhaps more general responses to political concerns over crime might be contained. But this obvious solution by no means is free of its own problems.

The first difficulty involves the identification of defendants as possibly unsafe risks for release. Statutory language is often too sweeping, and if pretrial release agencies were used to screen defendants beforehand, discretion simply would be moved to an earlier administrative process.

Another option is to release automatically all felony defendants under the custody of a pretrial release agency. The prosecutor then would be required to identify those who should have bail hearings as well as bearing the burden of proof to show why defendants should not be freed on recognizance.

Second, there is the critical problem at the conclusion of the hearing of what should be done regarding defendants judged to be highly likely to flee or to be grave threats to the safety of others. This ultimately raises, of course, the issue of preventive detention, and how rules can be drafted to prevent the abuse of this authority. Preventive detention is an issue about which there is little legal or political consensus. American reluctance to deal with it explicitly as a substitute for all forms of money bail after narrowing the role of bail hearings may mean, however, that more felony defendants will continue to incur punishment before trial than is necessary.

A Concluding Note on Ironies and Dilemmas

Ironies abound in American bail. One is that if punishment before trial is to be minimized for most felony defendants, it may be necessary to be more candid about the uses of bail as a means of preventive detention. This would elevate the importance of process and how decisions are made since the rationale for preventive detention would have to be clearly stated before taking such a step. If incarceration is the rare exception and not the general rule, the significance of the decision is heightened. This does not solve the problem of prediction, of course, but at a minimum a court record establishing the grounds for such decisions might begin to provide a basis for case law and review of bail decisions. Another irony is that ideological beliefs about bail satisfy those who hold them at the expense of defendants. As Thomas has observed:

> The present situation gives something to almost everybody. Liberals retain the belief that preventive detention is illegal, and risk of flight is the only permissible consideration in the setting of bail. Conservatives obtain a considerable amount of actual preventive detention. Detained defendants are clear losers but lack the muscle to change matters through the political process.[30]

There also is no scarcity of dilemmas. How can the bounds of preventive detention be limited? Is it possible to substitute preventive detention for existing bail practices? What guarantees are there that it would not be abused? These questions cannot be answered easily. By the same token, however, it must be recognized that current bail policies raise exactly the same issues, especially if bail reform continues. It is important to recall that the likelihood of detention tends to increase for defendants required to post money bail as the rate of recognizance rises. This may be due to either the declining performance of surety markets or the use of security bails to detain defendants. To what extent defendants under these conditions deliberately are detained as opposed to inadvertently jailed for want of sufficient resources to post bail is a question that raises issues of economic fairness as well as the legitimate use of bail. As incremental reform proceeds, it may create what Goldkamp calls "two classes of accused."[31] Several years ago Foote argued that a constitutional crisis was coming in American bail.[32] The irony is that its coming may be hastened because of bail reform.

REFERENCES

1. The information for 1973 is from the report done for District Court by the the National Council on Crime and Delinquency, *Pretrial Release in Maryland*, Hackensack, N. J., 1974, Table 8, p. 3.18. The recognizance and detention rates for 1976 are from the Lazar Institute, *Pretrial Release: An Evaluation of Defendant Outcomes and Program Impact*, Washington, D.C., 1981, Table 3, p. 6.
2. It should be mentioned that the meaning of "minimal" is relative to both court procedures and jail resources. Pretrial punishment still would vary across jurisdictions depending on what the courts perceived to be their maximum speed of disposition and the size of the jails. In addition, the fact that disposition slack has a less objective basis for measurement than detention resources has implications for the stability of disposition rates as will be seen shortly in the case of Detroit. For an argument that definitions of "court delay" reflect local legal cultures, see Thomas Church, Jr., *Justice Delayed: The Pace of Litigation in Urban Trial Courts*, Williamsburg, Va., National Center for State Courts, 1978.
3. This account is based on newspaper clippings and Recorder's Court's *Annual Reports* covering the years from 1974 through 1976.
4. *Detroit News*, January 28, 1976.
5. The composition of crimes against persons included felonious assault, murder, armed and unarmed robbery, and rape. In 1972 there were 1,115 defendants arraigned on armed robbery charges; in 1975 the number was 1,303. The number of rape defendants went from 139 to 358.
6. The full story is a bit more complicated than this brief account suggests. In 1972 three of the regular judges accounted for over half of all dispositions in Recorder's Court. The average presented here obscures this fact. In 1975 the court switched to a central assignment system after a period of internal conflict on the bench, and after this change the faster judges began to slow down. Finally, the visiting judge program ended after 1972, which reduced the personnel resources of the court.
7. Donald E. Pryor, "Pretrial Practices: A Preliminary Look at the Data," *Pretrial Issues*, Pretrial Services Resource Center, Washington, D.C., 1980, p. 1.
8. This simple "post hoc" comparison is used to make a point, not prove it. For a more sophisticated effort, see Roy B. Flemming, C. W. Kohfeld, and Thomas M. Uhlman, "The Limits of Bail Reform: A Quasi-Experimental Analysis," *Law and Society Review* 14 (Summer 1980): 947–976.

9. Stuart S. Nagel and Marian G. Neef, "The Policy Problem of Doing Too Much or Too Little: Pretrial Release as a Case in Point," in Stuart S. Nagel, and Marian G. Neef (eds.), *Legal Policy Analysis*, Lexington, Mass., Lexington Books, 1977.

10. Pryor, "Pretrial Practices," p. 14.

11. A useful review of the research on which the Manhattan Bail Project was based can be found in John S. Goldkamp, *Two Classes of Accused: A Study of Bail Detention in American Justice*, Cambridge, Ballinger Publishing Company, 1979.

12. Perhaps the only way of sorting out this issue, plus learning how court officials themselves perceive and weigh factors as they make bail decisions, would be to follow the methodology employed by Hogarth in his study of sentencing decisions. See John Hogarth, *Sentencing as a Human Process*, Toronto, University of Toronto Press, 1971.

13. See, for example, Arthur E. Angel, et al., "Preventive Detention: An Empirical Analysis," *Harvard Civil Rights—Civil Liberties Law Review* 6 (1971): 303–396; and John Monahan and Lesley Cummings, "Social Policy Implications of the Inability to Predict Violence," *Journal of Social Issues* 31 (1975): 153–164.

14. Chris W. Eskridge, "An Empirical Study of Failure to Appear Rates among Accused Offenders," *Pretrial Services Annual Journal* 2 (1979): 105–117.

15. Michael R. Gottfredson, "An Empirical Analysis of Pre-Trial Release Decisions," *Journal of Criminal Justice* 2 (1974): 287–303; also Michael B. Kirby, "Effectiveness of the Point Scale," Washington, D.C., Pretrial Service Resources Center, 1977 (mimeo).

16. For a discussion of the problems of predicting successes versus failures, see Lazar Institute, *Pretrial Release*, pp. 17 and 21.

17. Pryor, "Pretrial Practices," p. 20.

18. Various reform premises, including the "technocratic," are discussed by Raymond T. Nimmer, *The Nature of System Change: Reform Impact in Criminal Courts*, Chicago, American Bar Association, 1978.

19. National Center for State Courts, *Policymakers' Views Regarding Issues in the Operation and Evaluation of Pretrial Release and Diversion Programs*, Denver, National Center for State Courts, 1975, p. 40.

20. Obviously, the reverse situation could apply with a "reform" court setting the pace for the pretrial release agency. The point remains that it is the court that sets the priorities.

21. A discussion of the conditions affecting the impact of optional and mandatory reforms can be found in Nimmer, *Nature of System Change*, pp.186–192.

22. Lazar Institute, *Pretrial Release*, p. A.2.

23. Nimmer, *Nature of System Change*, p. 177 (emphasis in original).

24. Nimmer, p. 177.

25. The judge can be viewed as the commissioners' only "active constituency," an important factor in the success of optional reforms, see Nimmer, p. 188.

26. Nimmer, pp. 30–31.

27. Demeanor in open court was found to be statistically important in the decision to grant recognizance release and in the size of bail amounts, see Charles E. Frazier, E. Wilbur Bock, and John C. Henratta, "Pretrial Release and Bail Decisions," *Criminology* 18 (1980): 162–181.

28. Suzann R. Thomas Buckle and Leonard G. Buckle, *Bargaining for Justice*, New York, Praeger Publishers, 1977, pp. 74–80.
29. J. A. Gilboy, "The Dilemma of Seeking Bail and Preparing a Defense in Murder Cases," *Journal of Criminal Law and Criminology* 67 (1977): 259–272.
30. Wayne H. Thomas, Jr., *Bail Reform in America*, Berkeley, University of California Press, 1976, p. 247.
31. Goldkamp, *Two Classes of Accused*.
32. Caleb Foote, "The Coming Constitutional Crisis in Bail," *University of Pennsylvania Law Review* 113 (1965): 959–999, 1125–1185.

Appendix

RESEARCH METHODS

The methodology of this study was shaped by a concern with the process by which bails were set and with the context of this process. Accordingly, an eclectic approach was used to gather that data. Observation in the courtroom, interviews with officials and other actors, and the two samples of felony defendants drawn from Eisenstein and Jacob's study, *Felony Justice*, provided much of the data. This information was supplemented by newspaper articles and editorials, annual reports, and by published and unpublished documents, studies, and reports.

Observations of the bail hearings in Detroit and Baltimore were conducted to determine who participated in the hearings, their patterns of interaction, the "styles" of the officials, and the time devoted to the hearings. In December 1972 preliminary observations of two eight-hour shifts with Baltimore's District Court commissioners were conducted. These observations laid the basis for the preparation of a form used for the subsequent field work in June-July 1973 and May 1974 (see Exhibit 1). Later on a more elaborate form was developed for Detroit based on the experience in Baltimore (see Exhibit 2).

While it was hoped these forms would provide a way of recording information systematically they were not used in every instance for several reasons. For one thing, the forms were too elaborate, especially in Detroit. Also, much of the information was often missing at the hearings, particularly in Baltimore, or when available the participants did not verbalize their concerns or comment on the information during the hearings, which did not mean necessarily that it was unimportant. The forms furthermore were designed originally on the assumption that the hearings were discrete, bounded events. But oftentimes what transpired before and afterward was equally or more important. This was especially the case in Baltimore. Finally, as more hearings were observed it became apparent that the style and content of the questions, statements, and comments made by the actors would be lost if the forms were closely followed. It was not long before the backs of the forms were filled with more interesting and useful information than the fronts. Consequently, heavy reliance ultimately was placed on notes describing what happened during the hearings and including as close as possible verbatim statements of the participants. These notes were then used to reconstruct the events and activities surrounding each hearing and the hearings themselves shortly after each foray into the field.

Observations in Baltimore were conducted in all nine district court locations during both the evening and morning shifts and on weekends. Generally, the entire eight-hour shift was observed. The amount of time spent with the commissioners and the relatively small number of bail hearings and warrant requests left a great deal of time to develop rapport with these officials. We often had lunch or breakfast together and in one instance, despite personal qualms, left the district court for two hours with a commissioner and pretrial release investigator to attend a party at four o'clock in the morning. Whenever pretrial release investigators were present time was spent with them observing how they conducted interviews and verified the information, and talking with them about the Pre-Trial Release Division and their relations with the commissioners.

In Detroit, arraignments and bail hearings were held in a single courtroom and conducted twice a day during the week and once on weekends and holidays. Except for several weekends, almost all of the regularly scheduled arraignment sessions during the last week of June, all of July, and the first week of August 1974 were observed.

Unlike Baltimore where the commissioners were easily accessible before and after a bail hearing, access to Detroit's judges was more restricted. Becasue of their other court duties there was often little time to discuss their decisions with them before or after arraignments. Also, in contrast to Baltimore, the number of hearings held during a single session was large and they were processed more rapidly, making it difficult for the judges to recall in detail specific cases. Consequently, it was more difficult to learn the backgrounds and considerations of particular cases, aside from comments made during the hearings, unless there was some notable feature about a case which made it easier for the judge to remember it, e.g., the "beard" case.

Another effect of this difference was that interviews in Detroit were usually conducted separately from the observations. After an initial introduction and brief chat it was frequently necessary to arrange to see the judge at a later date when he or she had more time. In Baltimore observations and interviews were intermingled. An advantage of this situation was that the more general concerns of the interview agenda· could be related more closely with specific cases. It was easier for the commissioner to illustrate a broader point by using as an example a case that had just been observed. This opportunity to relate the particular with the general, unfortunately, was often absent in Detroit. A further advantage of this blending of observations and interviews was the chance it afforded to check the statements or comments of the commissioners with observed hearings; a valuable way of at least partially validating or questioning these comments. Again, this was less feasible in Detroit.

The interviews served a number of purposes. Essentially, they were used to gather information about both the process of bail setting and the more general context of these decisions. During the interviews, the impressions gained through observations were checked with the officials to see if they were correct or had any bearing on the process. They were asked to explain how they made their decisions and what they considered to be important factors in them. Whenever earlier comments, suggesions of particular officials or more general considerations for most of new questions or problems, they were brought up during succeeding interviews to find out if the officials felt they were simply idiosyncratic opinions of particular officials or more generaly considerations for most of them. Depending upon their response, these items were either dropped or added to the list of questions. Officials were also used as informants to explain unobserved events or to assess the role and importance of other actors who rarely were seen in the courtrooms. Finally, the interviews were a source of referrals to other persons or organizations the official thought should be interviewed.

Interviews were conducted in a varied manner ranging from semistructured to quite casual conversations depending upon the circumstances of the interviews. In Baltimore a form was prepared to guide the questioning (see Exhibit 3). For the most part, this form was used as a preliminary agenda of concerns which were raised with the commissioners. It also formed the basis for many of the questions asked in Detroit. Generally, however, the officials in both cities were allowed as much latitude as time permitted to develop in detail their responses and to raise problems unforeseen at the time of the form's preparation. Probing was extensively employed to flesh out their remarks or to challenge comments. In other words, interviews with officials were held in such a manner that the value of serendipity would not be lost. Whenever possible, comments which seemed to hold promise for new insights or information were not ignored. It would be difficult to report precisely the length of the interviews with the commissioners; the entire eight-hour shift constituted an extended interview. In Detroit, because they were usually separated from the observation stage, the interviews took from 30 minutes to two hours and averaged about an hour.

The least structured interviews were held with bondsmen, attorneys, pretrial release investigators, prosecutors, representatives of groups, jail officials, and Baltimore judges. Before the interviews, a list of general or specific topics was prepared, but because the vantage points and roles of these actors were so varied and the topics changed as more was learned, no single list of questions can be presented. The length of the interviews also varied widely. Two and one-half days were spent observing, talking, and questioning Detroit's leading bondsman. A day was spent following a

Baltimore bondsman as he went about his business. The briefest interview was held with the prickly chief judge of Baltimore's Supreme Bench
who bristled when the effectiveness of bail reform in the city was questioned. The amount of time spent with these different actors depended on
the broadness or narrowness of the topic, the number of topics, and the
time and patience of the persons interviewed. In some instances, e.g., the
bondsmen or group representatives, return visits were made to clarify
earlier answers or to ask new questions. The setting for these interviews
ranged from judge's chambers, court hallways and private offices, to res-
taurants and street corners.

The methods used in collecting the two samples of felony defendants,
the limitations of the data, and how the samples were weighted for analysis are discussed by Eisenstein and Jacob in *Felony Justice*. The data from
the two samples clearly constituted the empirical core of this study. They
provided the basis for determining the bail setting policies of the courts,
the bail histories of defendants used to develop the pretrial punishment
profiles, the correlates of the bail decisions, and the market share of Detroit's bondsmen.

All three sources of data—observations, interviews, and the defendant samples—had one problem in common. Despite the richness and
depth they supplied in understanding how the bail systems worked in the
cities, they created a relatively narrow temporal and institutional perspective. In order to broaden this focus it was necessary to rely on a variety of
secondary data sources such as newspapers, annual reports, and previously published studies about the cities and their courts. The information
gleaned from these sources was then used to identify and reconstruct
events involving the local criminal justice systems and to establish differences in their political environments. In this way, it was possible to gain a
more dynamic and contextual view of the bail practices in the two cities; a
view which emphasized how the courts and their political environments
interacted over time and how the interactions affected the behavior of the
actors observed or interviewed during the study period.

Exhibit 1

Preliminary Bail Setting Observation Form

Date: Length of time: to   Number:

Charges: 1.   ROR   Bail:
          2.   Bail:
          3.   Bail:

                                                   Total:

Pretrial recommend: NP N Y: what:

    If no recommendation, why?

Nature of criminal incident:

Record: Arrests: Convictions: Charges:

Warrants: N   Y   Failure to Appear: N   Y   Prob/parole: N   Y

Age: Employed: N   Y   where: Years:

Earnings/wk: Years in city:

Living with: Marital status: Dependents:

Alcohol: Y N   Drugs: Y   N   Still: Y   N

Concerns of Commissioners:

Actions/demeanor of defendant:

Police present, talk to commissioner:

Commissioner know about police feelings:

Lawyer present, content of remarks:

Exhibit 2

Final Bail Setting Observation Form

BAIL HEARING INTERCHANGE CODE SHEET   Number:_____   Time:_____

Indicate <u>who</u> made the statement or comment. If more than one point is made,
enter the appropriate letter again.

PT - Pretrail Release   P - Prosecutor
C - Commissioner   DC - Defense Attorney
J - Judge   D - Defendant
                             O - Other

Item Content	Initiate By	Comment By	Ques. By	Answ. By
1. Statements concerning facts surrounding EVENT/CRIME	____	____	____	____
2. Statements <u>emphasizing</u> seriousness of the crime	____	____	____	____
3. Comments minimizing seriousness of the crime	____	____	____	____
4. Mention of <u>penalty</u> for original charge	____	____	____	____
5. Mention of <u>penalty</u> of other charges	____	____	____	____
6. Speculation of <u>probable sentence</u> Def will get	____	____	____	____
7. Statements linking disposition or bail decision to Def	____	____	____	____
8. Comments regarding use of bail for <u>plea bargaining</u> purposes	____	____	____	____
9. Statements on <u>cooperativeness</u> of Def with prosecutor	____	____	____	____
10. Description of Def's PRIOR RECORD without judgment of "badness"	____	____	____	____

Item Content	Initiate By	Comment By	Ques. By	Answ. By
11. Statement <u>emphasizing seri-</u> <u>ousness</u> of prior record	___	___	___	___
12. Statement <u>minimizing seri-</u> <u>ousness</u> of prior record	___	___	___	___
13. Statements regarding in- formation about NATURE OF DEFENDANT	___	___	___	___
14. FAVORABLE comments on life circumstances, characteristics of Def	___	___	___	___
15. UNFAVORABLE comments on life circumstances, characteristics of Def	___	___	___	___
16. Comments regarding attitude (FAV, UNFAV) of <u>employer</u>	___	___	___	___
17. Comments of cooperation, attitudes of <u>family, rela-</u> <u>tives</u> of Def	___	___	___	___
18. Statements regarding Def's <u>likelihood of FTA</u>	___	___	___	___
19. Statements concerning Def's <u>threat</u> to victim, witnesses, community	___	___	___	___
20. Comments on Def's <u>ability</u> <u>to post</u> bail	___	___	___	___
21. Statements on <u>time spent by</u> <u>Def in jail</u> because of bail	___	___	___	___
22. Statement stressing <u>strength</u> of evidence vs. Def	___	___	___	___
23. Statement stressing <u>weakness</u> of evidence vs. Def	___	___	___	___
24. Statement that case is good (strong) for <u>prosecution</u>	___	___	___	___
25. Statement that case is good (strong) for <u>defense</u>	___	___	___	___

Item Content	Initiate By	Comment By	Ques. By	Answ. By
26. Statement regarding type of <u>representation</u>--assigned or PD	——	——	——	——
27. Statement regarding Def attempt to <u>delay</u>, not get DC, etc.	——	——	——	——
28. Comment on length of <u>time to trial</u>, trial date set.	——	——	——	——
29. Reference to establish <u>policies</u>, limits on type of release	——	——	——	——

Exhibit 3

Initial Baltimore Interview Form for Commissioners

Birthdate:_____   Date became commissioner:_____

What did you do before becoming a commissioner?   How long?

Compared to when first a commissioner using <u>ROR</u> less, more, same? Why?

What about <u>bail</u>? Less, same, more? Level of bail. Lower, same, higher? Why?

Ever use <u>security</u>? Often, some, never? Why? Advantages? Disadvantages?

<u>Information</u>: Too much, enough, too little? If too little, what? Why?

Where can you go for more information? How cooperative?

How frequently is this a problem? Very, often, not often.

What about felonies? How is that?

In reviewing a felony case, what do you look for in particular? What is important? Does it depend on the charge? How? (<u>Nature of offense</u>):

    Robbery:

    Burglary:

    Asslt w/i:

    Narcotics:

<u>Record</u>: If one, what do you look for? Most important? Anything most impt. as far as you are concerned? What is that?

Does it depend on the charge?

<u>Def. Background</u>: How adequate for you is PTR investigation? Very, Ade, Not.
How is that?

Anything in particular you look for? Why? What does it show?

If bail, how much weight to <u>ability to pay</u> premium? Major, Minor, Equal. Why?

If many could not make bail, should revisions be made for this? Y   N   Why?

As far as you know, what are <u>jail</u> conditions like? Crowded? Other aspects?

Should overcrowding be considered in decision?   Y   N   Why?

If cash bail is necessary, any kind of <u>initial amount</u> used in making decision?
Y   N

If yes: What about--

Robbery:

Burglary:

Asslt w/i:

Narcotics:

If no: How go about getting a figure?

Ever release a Def who was <u>rearrested</u>? How find out? What happened?

<u>Bail crime</u>: Who is concerned? How much? Very, some, little, none? Why?

Public:

Police:

Judges:

Media:

Some say <u>threat to community</u> (witness, etc.), how about you? Take it into consideration?   Y   N   Why?   How?   What do you look for?

Ever have a Def you released on bail or ROR <u>FTA</u>?   Y   N   What happened? How did you find out?

More likely with a felony? How is that?

<u>Bail Review</u>: Do you know when, if, a judge changes one of your decisions? Have you known of cases when this has happened? What did you do?

<u>Pretrial</u>: How useful personally in making your decision? Very, some, little? What is that?

   What about ROR?

   What about bail amounts?

   When do you find it necessary to reject PTR rec? Very often, often, some, infrequently? What is that?

   After a while do you find you can pretty much trust PTR?   Y   N   If yes, most of the time? If no, why?

   Is it a matter of getting to know the PTR? How is that? In what ways? How long does it take?

Do you feel that the police pretty much accept the commissioner system? How?

   What about your own relations? What kind of problems?

<u>Rule 777</u>: How well understood? How do you interpret it?

Index